Netaji
Living Dangerously

KINGSHUK NAG

PARANJOY

Published by Paranjoy Guha Thakurta

paranjoy@gmail.com

ISBN: 978-9-38443-969-9

© Kingshuk Nag, 2016

Kingshuk Nag asserts the moral right to be identified as the author of this work.

First Edition

Typeset in Adobe Jenson Pro 11/14.5 by Ram Das Lal, NCR Delhi

Cover design: PealiDezine

Publishing Facilitation: AuthorsUpFront

All rights reserved. No part of this publication may be reproduced, stored in a retrieval system, or transmitted, in any form or by any means, without the prior written permission of the AUTHOR, or as expressly permitted by law, or under terms agreed with the appropriate reprographic rights organisations. Enquiries concerning reproduction outside the scope of the above should be sent to the AUTHOR.

In memory of my father, Dr Salil Kumar Nag.
Like many of his generation, he earnestly believed
that under the leadership of Netaji Subhas Chandra Bose,
India would have been a different country
when it gained political Independence.

And in memory of my friend and colleague, Sumit Sen,
Resident Editor, *The Times of India*, Kolkata,
who tried to unravel the mysteries about Netaji with zeal,
till cancer snatched him away suddenly in September 2015.

Contents

	Preface	vii
	Introduction: The Pilgrim's Progress	1
1.	The Air Crash Story	20
2.	Surrendering to the Russians	30
3.	Stalin, Nehru and Netaji	40
4.	Why Nobody Lobbied for Netaji's Freedom	51
5.	The Rise of Subhas	63
6.	Gandhi Coterie and Subhas Bose	77
7.	Escape from Calcutta	88
8.	In Hitler's Germany	98
9.	INA and Azad Hind Government	109
10.	Nehru, Mountbatten and Freedom	121
11.	Divided Bengal	133
12.	The Mystery of Gumnami Baba	146
13.	The Transformation	160
14.	Was Netaji Forsaken by His Own Government?	155
	About the Author	183

Preface

Satyameva Jayate, truth alone triumphs, is the national motto of India. But sadly this motto—drawn from the *Mundaka Upanishad*—is often not acted upon. The mystery behind the disappearance of Netaji Subhas Chandra Bose and the diminution of the exceptional role he played in India's independence movement is a striking example of how truth has deliberately been prevented from triumphing.

But every night has a dawn and this long dark night where Netaji was relegated to the ash heap of history, with the truth of his disappearance perhaps hidden in secret government records, is about to end.

The first salvo has been fired by the Chief Minister of West Bengal, Mamata Banerjee, who bit the bullet and ordered declassification of sixty-four files relating to Netaji that were in the custody of the West Bengal state intelligence department. Releasing the files in the middle of September 2015, she said that from a reading of the documents it was clear that Netaji had lived beyond 1945. By doing this she created history because this is the first official statement confirming the survival of Netaji beyond 18 August 1945. Of course, the Justice Manoj Kumar Mukherjee Commission of Inquiry into Netaji's disappearance had also said in its report submitted in 2005 that he could not have died in the air crash on that fateful day because there was no evidence of such a crash. But the report was rejected by the Union government in New Delhi. The files opened by Mamata add up to a staggering 12,744 pages and they have now been kept for public viewing at the Police Museum in Kolkata.

The declassification of the files has had a salutary effect: pressure has mounted on the Union government to open up the files in its custody—including those in the Prime Minister's Office (PMO). Not only have relatives of Netaji stepped up their campaign but so have other private groups like the Rashtriya Sainik Sanstha (an organization comprising civilian patriots and more than one lakh ex-servicemen). Retired intelligence officials, their lips sealed even after superannuation, have started speaking out even if in off-the-record conversations. All of which is throwing more light on the Netaji mystery.

On 14 October 2015 talking to thirty-five family members of Netaji who had called on him in a much publicized meeting, Prime Minister Narendra Modi said that he found no reason for the Netaji files to remain secret and announced that paying heed to requests made by Netaji's relatives, the Government of India would start declassifying them beginning 23 January 2016. This will be the 120th birthday of the patriot. Modi also said that he would write to foreign governments—beginning with Russia in December—to declassify any Netaji-related files that they might have in their archives. He said that the other countries to be approached would include the United Kingdom, USA, Japan, China, Singapore and Malaysia. Later Modi tweeted that 'there is no need to strangle history. Nations that forget their history lack the power to create it'. Independent researchers till date have faced huge barriers while dealing with foreign governments. They have repeatedly been told that a government-to-government request might yield better results. But all previous Indian governments have preferred to remain silent. If the current Indian government acts on the prime minister's statement and puts in a request to foreign governments it might well induce the latter to part with information.

Thirteen of the declassified files reveal the shocking fact that Netaji's close relatives were subjected to round-the-clock surveillance by intelligence sleuths with their mail being intercepted on a regular basis. This included correspondence received as well as sent out by members of the Bose family. A team of fourteen sleuths were deployed for this purpose. This was an incredibly large and complex operation and had obviously been mounted because the intelligence department was keen to trace Netaji's whereabouts. The operation was carried on till the late 1960s, confirming that they believed that he had not died till then. While the government deployed this massive intelligence operation, the official committees set up to investigate the disappearance of Netaji were being encouraged to report that he had died in the air crash, which now seems to not have happened at all.

These declassified intelligence files reveal that the sleuths were searching far and wide for Netaji and had even been examining a lead that he had escaped from Singapore at the end of World War II in a submarine. They were also trying to figure out whether he had escaped to China and mingled with Mao Zedong's forces. The Chinese angle may have caught the fancy of the intelligence community because close relatives of Netaji were themselves trying to investigate whether he had made it to China. On 5 March 1948, Chow Hsiang Kungg, apparently an Indian official, or perhaps an interpreter who worked out of the Old Secretariat in Delhi wrote to Amiya Nath Bose, son of Netaji's elder brother Sarat Chandra Bose informing him that a quick search of Chinese newspapers had not thrown up any leads that the leader was in Nanking (Nanjing). The letter was written in response to a specific query from Amiya. Addressed to his Calcutta (Kolkata) address, it never reached him since it was confiscated by intelligence at the post-office. Adding to the mystery was a report published in the tabloid *Blitz* on 26 March 1949 that Bose was alive in Red China. A few years later in 1956, Suresh Chandra Bose, another elder sibling of Netaji, wrote about the possibility of his brother's presence in China. In his dissenting report as a member of the Shah Nawaz Committee set up that year to investigate the circumstances of Netaji's death — but published independently—Suresh Bose wrote that two witnesses had submitted to the Committee that Netaji had made attempts at contacting the Chinese Communists through the Vietnamese Communist leader Ho Chi Minh. They had also placed on record that crossing over to Yan'an, Chinese leader Mao Zedong's headquarters, was one of the options considered by Netaji. Both witnesses were officers of the Indian National Army (INA)—an armed force formed by Indian nationalists in South-east Asia in 1942 and led by Netaji—of which Shah Nawaz Khan was also a senior member. Suresh Bose also cited evidence (that seemed stronger) that Netaji was trying to contact the Russians. In fact he concluded, 'it was their (Netaji's and the Japanese) joint and agreed plan that Netaji would finally move to Russian territory. In accordance with this plan, the Japanese government took Netaji to Manchuria from where he evidently moved into Russian territory'.

One of the declassified files reveals a Criminal Investigation Department (CID) report from Howrah that quotes a British and US intelligence filing that Netaji was alive after 1945 and 'might have undertaken training in Russia'. One of the files contains an intercepted letter dated 18 November 1949 written by Amiya Nath to his brother Sisir Kumar Bose that says, 'for the last one month we are getting this broadcast on the short wave near 16 mm. The broadcast only says Netaji Subhas Chandra Bose *transmittere kotha bolte cheyechen* (wants to transmit his message over the radio). This sentence is repeated for hours'. Other files from this lot show that between 1942 and 1945 there were a series of reports from intelligence agents that claimed that Netaji had perished in an air crash, but each time the leader was found to be alive.

The extensive surveillance on Bose had a political objective, according to a top official of the Intelligence Bureau (IB), who now lives a life of quiet retirement. 'Subhas Bose was alive and if he had appeared in India in the mid-1950s, Prime Minister Jawaharlal Nehru's position would be at risk. Subhas Bose had the charisma to win the elections and upstage Nehru. Thus the IB was deployed to find out where he was and what he was doing,' the officer told this writer, breaking his silence of many years.

Having served his entire career with the IB—from the early 1950s to the early 1990s—the officer was privy to many facts and said that it was none other than Bhola Nath Mullick, the director of IB for a record twenty years, who organized the surveillance. The official added that Mullick, who is dubbed as the father of the Indian intelligence service and served at the helm of the IB from 1948 to 1968, had the total trust of Nehru and 'could even lecture' the prime minister. Incidentally, Mullick hailed from the Shyambazar area of Kolkata, Netaji's hometown.

The snooping on relatives was carried out in the hope that wherever he was, Netaji would try and contact them. The tabs on the family were kept through the Calcutta office of the IB. The officer added that the IB believed that Bose was hiding either in the Soviet Union or Japan. The latter country had not been ruled out because he had last been seen on Japanese territory in Saigon. Although the regime changed after World War II, the Japanese Emperor continued to hold sway and so did top functionaries like the foreign minister, Mamoru Shegimitsu, who continued in that position until the mid-1950s, much after the Japanese defeat.

In the end, according to the retired official, the IB could never establish the whereabouts of Netaji.

Even as Netaji was lost to the world, some of his former associates were feted by the Nehru government and made hay as the sun shone. Shah Nawaz Khan, who headed the Committee which declared that Netaji had perished in the air crash in Taiwan, not only became a deputy minister in the central government but was apparently also allowed to set up a huge farm in Saharanpur district Uttar Pradesh. The farm was next to a reserve forest and there are allegations that he encroached on forest land as the government looked the other way. It seems that a railway station was established in the vicinity for Khan's benefit. Anand Mohan Sahay, part of Netaji's Azad Hind government became a diplomat in the Nehru regime. Strangely in his memoirs,

Stirring Times: An Autobiography of a Nationalist, the chapter on the INA period was compiled by his daughter and is a rather generalized account. She claimed that Sahay had lost his notes on the INA and so she had done the honours by referring to the remaining material she had encountered while staying with her father. But one gets the impression that this was a deliberate underplaying of one of the most important episodes of Sahay's life, possibly in order to negate Netaji's contributions.

Those who tried to reveal the truth about Netaji did come under pressure to desist from their quest. Suresh Bose in his *Dissentient Report* wrote, 'I regret very much to state that hindrances, obstructions and pressure were brought to bear on me by some of the highest government officials with the sole intention of making it impossible for me to write it. With that purpose in view and after I had dissented from the opinion of my colleagues, which was also the opinion of the prime minister, not a single piece of paper necessary for writing my report was given to me.' Suresh Bose's grandson Amit Mitra, the present finance and industry minister of West Bengal, remembers how Shah Nawaz Khan visited his grandfather at home to try and convince him not to dissent from the main report, which would declare that Subhas had died in the air crash.

Although it is possible that with renewed interest in Netaji's disappearance, the long-standing mystery will be solved, many think that the declassification of the files may not yield anything. In fact, the central government may have very few files which would throw light on the matter. India's first Chief Information Commissioner Wajahat Habibullah was quoted in various reports in the press in July and August 2015 that the bulk of files on Netaji in the custody of the PMO were unlikely to have survived. While he did not rule out a conspiracy, he speculated that they may have been 'lost' due to the poor record-keeping system in the PMO and government offices. He said that in his tenure he had come across many instances where government records could not be traced. Habibullah said that the government had accepted the plea that relations with Russia would be severely affected if the files were declassified.

The declassified files from West Bengal also have pages that are missing. West Bengal government sources claim that the pages have been missing for a long time and may have been damaged during an earlier regime. But a retired Indian Police Service (IPS) officer from West Bengal who had also served in the IB claimed that the files are sought to be kept secret because they contain 'many truths' that may 'expose the activities of important people whose reputation is still untainted'.

This IPS officer who had done a detailed study of Netaji during his intelligence days says that Subhas Chandra Bose was a man who was single-minded about securing freedom for India and that 'everything else was secondary for him'. The officer added: 'He was direct and did not beat around the bush. Because of this trait many thought he was arrogant. But this was not arrogance, it was only that he was supremely confident.'

Suresh Bose says that Subhas 'was made of different stuff and something above the ordinary. Religion was ingrained in him and love and sympathy for all living beings were part of his nature. Even as a boy, he was of a reserved, sober and thoughtful type who generally spent some time in meditation secretly'.

This is ultimately what made Subhas Chandra Bose the person he was.

Introduction

The Pilgrim's Progress

Sometime in late June 1993, Ronen Sen, then India's ambassador to Russia, was startled to hear from the Indologist Albert Belsky that the forthcoming issues of *Asia and Africa Today*, a bi-monthly journal devoted to social and political affairs, based in Moscow, would publish a series of articles portraying Subhas Chandra Bose as an agent of MI6 (the secret intelligence service of the British government responsible for gathering foreign intelligence, while the security service or MI5 is responsible for internal security). Sen was informed that the articles would be based on classified archival material belonging to the KGB (the intelligence arm of the government of the Soviet Union). Wary of the damaging consequences of the revelations, Sen wrote to the foreign secretary, Jyotindra Nath Dixit on 24 June 1993, informing him that a few Indian journalists in Moscow had got wind of the forthcoming stories. Sen also despatched Ajai Malhotra, then Information Counsellor at India's embassy in Moscow, to meet the deputy chief editor of the magazine V.K. Tourdjev, unearth the information he had about Bose and try to dissuade him from publishing scurrilous stories about the Indian patriot.

Malhotra met Tourdjev on 29 June 1993. The editor confirmed that his magazine would publish the articles, the first of which was to be titled 'The Secret Behind the Death of S.C. Bose'. He showed

Malhotra—though displayed at a distance—a letter dated 11 December 1943, marked 'Top Secret' and addressed to Colonel A.P. Osipov, a Soviet intelligence officer. Written by Colonel G.A. Hill of British intelligence, it said that Bose had 'cooperated' with MI6 and that one of his close associates was a KGB agent. Tourdjev told Malhotra that his contacts in the KGB had provided him with all the inputs for the planned articles and that he was exhibiting the communication as proof that the articles would be based on evidence.

Malhotra was also told that the articles would argue that Bose had escaped from house arrest in Calcutta in January 1941 and made his way to Kabul with the full knowledge of the British and that is why he could survive in the distant capital of Afghanistan for a whole month without being arrested by the security forces. None of Netaji's India-specific orders given out from Germany—like subversion activities on India's western frontier—were ever meant to be carried out. After all, it was all part of a British plan, with Bose acting on their orders.

Malhotra was rather alarmed and without delay, passed on a comprehensive note to Ambassador Sen who, in turn forwarded it to New Delhi for further action. The establishment in the Indian capital failed to gauge the importance of the information emanating from Moscow. They did not understand that Netaji had become the 'fall-guy' in a 'great game' between intelligence departments which have a penchant for planting misleading information in their quest to 'destroy' enemies.

The Indian establishment of the time seems to have been under the grip of the overarching thought—how would Indians react upon learning that Netaji was a British agent? It is ironic that the Indian government entertained the preposterous suggestion that Bose was an agent of the British Empire—throughout his life he had been its sworn enemy.

Thus, instead of taking up cudgels for one of India's greatest freedom fighters and asserting that the purported evidence against him had been circulated by the MI6 with an ulterior motive, the mandarins of South

Block and North Block of the Government of India's secretariat on New Delhi's Raisina Hill fell back on an old stratagem. They decided the best way to bring about a resolution to the disquieting information would be to prove once over that Netaji had, in fact, died in the air crash in Taiwan and that the ashes stored in an urn at Tokyo's Renkoji Temple was that of the patriot. This, it was hoped, would put a lid on the various theories around his disappearance at the end of World War II, once and for all. It would be like the Hindi epithet mouthed by Pran, who is famous for essaying the role of the quintessential villain in Bollywood movies: 'Naa rahe baans, na baje bansuri' (which, loosely translated, means, 'If there is no bamboo, how can a flute be fashioned?'). In effect, this meant that if the cause of action was taken away, would there be any action?

Towards this end, in October 1993 orders went out from Amar Nath Verma, principal secretary to Prime Minister P.V. Narasimha Rao to settle the controversy about Netaji's ashes before his birth centenary in January 1997. The home secretary, K. Padmanabhaiah tried hard to persuade members of the Bose family to accept that it was indeed Netaji's ashes that were stored at Renkoji Temple. A high-profile minister of the government also called on Emilie Schenkl, Netaji's widow who was then living in Germany, to accept once and for all that her illustrious husband had died in Taihoku (Taipei) airport.

Nothing came of the effort.

A few years later, when retired Supreme Court judge, Manoj Kumar Mukherjee—of the single-member Commission instituted in 1999 after a Calcutta High Court order to inquire into the disappearance of Netaji—demanded to see the related files, incumbent home secretary, Kamal Pande refused to part with them. Pande filed an affidavit with the Commission stating that the revelations in the files would lower the image of Netaji in the public eye and lead to public disorder besides affecting relations with friendly foreign countries. Till this date—in 2015—the Government of India has been chary about declassifying the files on the same plea. In reality Bose had shaken the confidence of the

British establishment when he escaped from house arrest in Calcutta late on the night of 16 or 17 January 1941, hoodwinking the intelligence agents stationed in large numbers outside the Bose home in Calcutta's tony Elgin Road. The sleuths had their informers within the house, the servants, but Bose had so meticulously planned his escape that very few knew of his audacious plan.

After his fallout with the Congress bosses in 1939, Bose—who had been elected president of the party, defeating the official candidate (who had the blessings of Mahatma Gandhi)—had to resign his position and leave the party. Even though the British sensed that Bose was on a weak wicket, they felt that he could not be trusted to lie low with World War II raging, unlike the other Congress worthies who seemed willing to support the War effort. Bose was arrested and packed off to Calcutta's Alipore Presidency Jail, the British hoping to keep him imprisoned till the end of the War.

Subhas Bose had a robust personality and was not one who would have passively accepted a situation of enforced inaction. He would soon devise a way out of jail. As part of his plan, he went on an indefinite hunger strike and allowed his health to deteriorate. The British administration went into one big scare. Afraid of antagonizing Indians if something were to happen to Bose while in jail, the administration released him and put him under house arrest in his family home in the city. From here, he gave his jailers the slip. The sleuths posted outside the house had no clue that Bose had manoeuvred his way out and escaped. They were under the impression that he was at home but had withdrawn into the recesses of his room for spiritual exercises. That Subhas was spiritually inclined was known to all. When, ten days after his escape, family members declared Subhas missing, he was crossing over the frontier between India and Afghanistan, having travelled incognito on a long train journey that took him from Calcutta to Peshawar. From Afghanistan he intended to cross the border into the Soviet Union.

The British still had no clue about Bose's whereabouts and their first instinct was that he had boarded a ship out of Calcutta and was headed to Japan. Later they figured out that he could be on his way to Germany. Immediately instructions were issued to the Special Operations Executive—a war-time irregular force created on the orders of British Prime Minister Winston Churchill for various subversive activities—to execute Bose on sight. The British expected Bose to cross over to Germany via Istanbul and planned to target him there. As it turned out, Bose's first choice was not Germany, but the Soviet Union.

The 1917 October Revolution in Russia had raised hopes amongst the underdogs of the world and Bose—though not a Communist—believed that for India to move forward in a progressive manner, feudal forces would have to be eliminated through land redistribution in tandem with the growth of modern industries, in a planned manner. In fact, as Congress President, he had set up the Planning Committee, forerunner to the Planning Commission instituted after Independence. In fact, Bose ran afoul with the coterie that controlled the Congress because of his radical ideas: he wanted genuine reforms in land relations but the party bosses were quite content to merely replace the British as new masters of the country. They were not willing to destabilize the status quo beyond pushing out the British and did not seem inclined to push through reforms.

From Kabul Bose tried hard to cross the border into the Soviet Union but failed. At that time, although Germany was still not at war with the Soviet Union—a non-aggression pact had been signed by the foreign ministers of the two countries—there were some expectations that this would soon be breached.

More importantly Soviet intelligence was spreading rumours that the Red Army would attack India from its north-west border and liberate it. When it was learnt that Bose could also be trying to push into the Soviet Union, British apprehensions became more pronounced which they countered with rumours that they would attack Baku in southern Soviet Union. Now in Azerbaijan, the city on the western coast of the Caspian Sea was the Soviet Union's energy and oil hub. The Soviets then developed cold feet about granting refuge to Bose fearing that it would strengthen the feeling that an India invasion plan was on. All Bose could manage was a transit visa through Soviet territories on the way to Germany, which was valid for a very short period, 23–31 March 1941. Even this visa came to him courtesy the Italians, who had a better opinion of him than the Germans.

Adolf Hitler was obsessed with the British—his declarations of hostilities notwithstanding—he aspired to be like them. He believed that the Asiatic races and non-Aryans were inferior races and had declared this in *Mein Kampf*, the autobiographical manifesto published in two volumes in 1925 and 1926 respectively. The German leader was so race conscious that he allowed the 1936 Olympic Games to be held in Berlin only to prove white race supremacy. As it turned out, the African-American athlete Jesse Owens dominated the tracks and won numerous gold medals and a fuming Hitler stomped out of the stadium. Bose, who had earlier sojourned in Austria for a long period, had condemned Hitler's views on race in a press conference and demanded withdrawal of these views.

Thus Bose would have expected that things would not be very smooth in Germany. When the Germans attacked the Soviet Union on 22 June 1941, less than three months after his reaching Berlin, Bose realized that his options had been severely curtailed. He voiced his protest against the German incursions into the Soviet Union and refused to be cowed down, although he was, metaphorically speaking, in the lion's den. He said that in India there were sympathies for the Soviet Union among the people and the German invasion would be viewed adversely in his country.

Though the Indian cause did not mean much to Hitler, his intelligence reports had suggested that Bose was a popular figure in his own country and had great potential. Thus he was willing to tolerate Bose and to even provide financial assistance to set up the Free India Legion. Hitler also had no objection to handing over Indian prisoners of war (POW) of the British Indian Army to Bose for retraining and deployment in a future invasion of India. A Free India Radio to beam Bose's messages fortnightly was also permitted.

Bose's rhetoric was decidedly anti-imperialist. Bose also did something in Berlin that was sacrilege for Hitler: he lived openly with his Austrian partner Emilie Schenkl, whom he was introduced to in Vienna. In Hitler's Germany, inter-racial marriages and cohabitation was strictly prohibited. But Bose could not care less and Hitler seems to have looked the other way. Apparently they married secretly in 1937 in a Hindu ceremony though there is no civil record. They seem to have married in the *gandharva* tradition of ancient India, which is based on mutual attraction between a man and a woman. They would have probably got together, exchanged garlands and simply declared themselves man and wife. Their daughter Anita was born in November 1942.

There were liberals in Hitler's establishment who, unlike the Führer, saw India as a country with a rich and ancient culture. They were willing to patronise and protect Bose in a country where there was no rule of law. There was always the danger of Bose being picked up and despatched to a Nazi concentration camps and exterminated. In fact, one of Bose's closest supporters Friedrich Adam von Trott zu Solz, an important functionary in the German foreign office was hanged in 1944—along with many others—for being part of a plan to oust Hitler. By then Bose had left Germany.

Whatever assistance Hitler's regime might have been giving to Bose, Hitler himself was not willing to meet the Indian leader, who was kept under constant surveillance. Bose had to wait a year for an appointment which came about in May 1942. The meeting turned out to be a near disaster with Bose reiterating his demand that Hitler withdraw objectionable sections from *Mein Kampf* and the Führer launching into an extended monologue.

Bose was, however, able to convince Hitler to facilitate his move to the Far East, and was to transfer to South-east Asia in an epic underwater journey in a German submarine. The journey involved a submarine-to-submarine transfer mid-ocean, with Bose and an associate transferring from the German U-boat to a Japanese submarine near the Indian Ocean island of Madagascar.

After the long and hazardous journey which he risked with equanimity, Bose disembarked on a small island in Japanese-held Sumatra in May 1943, and was ultimately to reach Tokyo. Bose, who had begun to be hailed as Netaji by his followers, was obsessed with the idea of a free India and spent all his waking hours thinking of how to break the shackles that bound his motherland.

Bose's appearance in Tokyo and the warm welcome shown to him by the imperial Japanese government set alarm bells ringing in His Majesty's Government. British intelligence agencies began to conjure various strategies to foil Bose's plans. This resulted in a nefarious plot to portray him as a British agent. Of course, the agencies knew that describing Bose in this way would draw derision all round. Thus, in the usual fashion of intelligence agencies, they resorted to a cloak and dagger game.

When Bose arrived in Tokyo and even after he had moved to Singapore to head the Indian National Army (INA), Japan was not at war with the Soviet Union, the two countries having entered into a non-aggression pact in April 1941. Engaged in intense hostilities with Germany on their western front, the Soviets did not want to be hemmed in from the rear by the Japanese. At the zenith of its power, Japan had never lost a war till then. It had occupied Manchuria on the border of the Soviet Union and what is more, had given a bloody nose to Russia in conflicts in the earlier part of the twentieth-century.

It did not take much for British intelligence to figure out that Bose would contact the Joseph Stalin regime. Their field reports must have also indicated that Bose was trying to contact the Soviet leadership via their ambassador in Tokyo, Yakov Alexandrovich Malik (who was known as Jacob Malik in the non-Soviet world). So the best way to sow doubts about Bose among the Soviets was to portray a confused picture of his intent. Through inferences and suggestions, fabricated documents and misleading leads, Bose was made out to be a British agent. Of course, projecting outright that Bose was a paid agent of MI6 would not wash. The Soviets were not foolish enough to fall for this bait. Yet, this attempt was a subtle one, enough to create apprehensions in the minds of the Soviets.

During World War II a large part of the Soviet administration had moved to Omsk in Siberia to be far away from the Germans. It is here that Netaji despatched his representative to establish a consulate of the Arzi Hukumat-e-Azad Hind (Provisional Government of Free India). The representative—Kato Kochu—went without proper credentials. History does not record Kato's identity. In all probability he was an Indian with an assumed Japanese identity. Netaji had already written to Jacob Malik—a copy of that letter was recently declassified from the KGB archives.

And it is Omsk that Netaji sought to travel to once it seemed that the end of the War was imminent and the Japanese would surrender. On 18 August 1945, when Bose took off from Saigon supposedly en route to Tokyo, he was actually headed for Omsk. His immediate destination was Dairen (Dalian) in Manchuria, which until the end of the War was under Japanese occupation with a puppet regime. Manchuria was captured by the Soviets after the atom bomb was dropped on Hiroshima and Nagasaki even as they declared War on the Japanese on 9 August 1945. Netaji wanted to surrender to the Red Army in Dairen in the hope that he would be allowed to establish the headquarters of the Azad Hind government in Omsk. This is why Bose went into Soviet territory with two trunks full of Azad Hind treasure. The treasure—which was the sum total of the donations that he had received in South-east Asia—would meet the monetary needs of the government. However, Netaji had more treasures with him, from the INA, but could not carry them all because the Japanese bomber which ferried him had reached its weight limit. The remaining treasure was left back in Saigon and to give an impression that there was actually an air crash a part of it was taken to Tokyo. It was suggested that this was recovered from the wrecked aircraft. We will return to the story of the INA treasure later in this chapter.

For Bose entering Soviet Russia was a leap of faith into the unknown, a step fraught with many imponderables. What he would not have known was that British intelligence had foreseen his possible course of action and had probably poisoned the minds of the Soviets against him already. This was not a difficult feat, as Stalin and his men knew very little about India. Stalin's knowledge of India was particularly appalling—he was confused as to whether the primary language of India was Gujarati or Hindi and was under the impression that the island nation of Ceylon was a part of India. Stalin had a poor opinion about Indian Congress leaders who he believed were stooges of the British. He seems to have been misinformed that they were merely fighting for limited independence and that this stance would lead to a continuance of indirect British rule in India with the British Army continuing to protect Indian territories. In Soviet intelligence dossiers Bose was described as coming from a huge landholding feudal family. This was hardly expected to endear him to Stalin, a man with a fetish for collectivisation of agriculture.

It is true though that after India's Independence, some Soviet representatives observing the country had identified Bose as a leader that they could work with because of his radical views. Even if this could have persuaded Stalin to look favourably at Bose, it was undone by British reports that described him as their agent. The secret ways of Bose and his changing stances in choosing partners—its sole objective being the service of the nation—was something that could be understood only by his countrymen. But for outsiders this raised suspicions about Bose's actual motives. Bose did not have any friends within the Kremlin who could have allayed the misapprehensions of the regime. He was depending on his luck, audacity and sincerity of purpose. But the deceitful British had already played their games. What harmed Bose was that his trusted man on the Afghan frontier, Bhagat Ram Talwar gave away his plans. Subhas Bose had depended on Talwar for assistance in crossing the frontier into Soviet territory. But unknown to Bose, Ram was a double agent—spying for both Great Britain and the Soviet Union. The Soviets knew that he was periodically double-crossing them. If Bose was using such a man for his purpose, then could he be depended upon?

Although the British, Russians and Americans were on the same side during World War II, there was considerable mutual distrust. In this scenario it was possible that even a figure like Netaji could be discredited by the Russians as a British agent and made to pay. In fact Bose was not the only person to have been penalized in this manner. The most well-known example is that of the Swedish diplomat Raoul Gustaf Wallenberg who was posted to Budapest during the War. The third Reich held sway in Hungary and Wallenberg had been going out of the way to prevent thousands of Jews from being despatched to extermination camps. This he did by issuing Swedish passports to Jews in trouble. In January 1945, the Soviets walked into Budapest and captured Austria. They arrested Wallenberg the day they entered Budapest on charges that he was an American spy. Wallenberg was swallowed up behind the Iron Curtain, never to emerge again. Many years later, under intense Swedish pressure the Soviet government did admit that the diplomat had perished in a Moscow prison.

In the run up to India's Independence Jawaharlal Nehru had started wooing the powers-that-be in the Soviet Union. In 1946 he wrote a letter to Stalin and gave it to Soviet agent V.G. Sayadiants who was based in Bombay (Mumbai) and was known to be the eyes and ears of Moscow. The contents of the letter are not known but Nehru requested Sayadiants that he hand it over to Stalin personally. Once an interim government had been appointed in 1946, Nehru tried to approach the Soviet regime with the help of V.K. Krishna Menon, a known Communist who was later to be his defence minister. Nehru also appointed his sister Vijayalakshmi Pandit as the first Indian ambassador to the Soviet Union. Interestingly in his report to Stalin, Sayadiants had spoken glowingly about Gandhi and approvingly of

Nehru but advised that the Soviets could work with Bose and the Forward Bloc, which Bose had founded.

India's relationship with Soviet Russia never warmed up while Stalin was alive—notwithstanding great efforts by Nehru through Indian ambassadors Sarvepalli Radhakrishnan and K.P.S. Menon. The ambassadors made a strong pitch for India, arguing that the new Republic of India would follow a similar trajectory to that of the Soviet Union—India was also modelled as a socialist secular republic—but to no avail. India's relations with the Soviet Union developed into a close and cosy arrangement only after the death of Stalin in 1953.

In all probability Bose was held in a gulag, the massive system of forced labour camps found in Siberia during the time of Stalin. He was probably kept alive because the Soviets wanted to use him for furthering Soviet interests in India if required. He had been dispatched to the gulag after some internal discussions. Bose's credentials possibly came into question as a result of the false rumours against him spread by British intelligence. By implication, when the Soviets built their long-lasting relationship with India after 1955 it was by sacrificing the cause of Subhas Bose. By 1957, the Swedes had been able to get an official confirmation from the Soviets that Raoul Wallenberg had been in their custody. But the Indian government did nothing to obtain information about Netaji.

On the contrary efforts were made to prove that Netaji had died in the air crash at Taihoku on 18 August 1945. The committee headed by Shah Nawaz Khan—who had by then become a minister in Nehru's government—concluded that Netaji had indeed died in that fateful air crash even as Suresh Bose published his dissenting view. Meanwhile the Indian government's Intelligence Bureau (IB) began tailing Netaji's relatives in India and reading their correspondence. Obviously the IB was trying to figure out whether the relatives who were making their own enquiries about Bose's fate were getting closer to unravelling the mystery behind the disappearance of the great patriot. It may be noted that although India was free, the IB–which was a legacy from the British times—maintained very close relations with MI5. (Years later, in 2010, the official historian of the MI5 would wonder whether Nehru knew all that was going on behind his back.)

The INA treasures were also used to 'prove' that Netaji had died in the air crash. In 1952 Nehru formally declared in Parliament that Subhas Bose had expired in the crash and quoted Subbier Appadurai Ayer—the Azad Hind government's information minister—to buttress this claim. Ayer, who by then had become director of publicity of Bombay State (comprising the Bombay Presidency and adjoining princely states) in independent India was sent to Tokyo in 1951, ostensibly to investigate the whereabouts of the INA treasures lying there. There was a lot of controversy because the Indians living there—believed that M. Ramamurthy, who was the chief of the Indian Independence League, had pilfered the treasures and shared the booty with the British intelligence officer Lieutenant Colonel John George Figgess (who subsequently became an an expert on oriental curios). Ayer was believed to be extremely close to Ramamurthy and his arrival in Tokyo angered the Indian community. The head of the Indian liaison mission in Tokyo, K.K. Chettur, in a communication had offered to probe the disappearance of the treasure. At that time Ram Chandra Dattatraya Sathe, an under-secretary in the external affairs ministry (later foreign secretary) wrote in a note that Ayer had brought 11 kg of gold plus 3 kg of gold mixed with molten iron from Saigon to the Japanese capital in 1945. Ayer was with Netaji when he left for Dairen but could not board the aircraft due to lack of space. When Ayer was quizzed in Tokyo in 1951 he declared that he had left the treasure with Ramamurthy, but the popular belief was that he possessed more information than he had revealed about the fate of the treasure. After Ayer returned to India and testified that indeed Netaji had died in an air crash he was appointed as advisor, integrated publicity programme for Nehru's five-year plans.

The Indian public did not take kindly to the attempts made by the

Indian government to prove that Netaji was dead. He had achieved a cult status in the country by then and many people—especially in his home state of Bengal—expected him to surface anytime and deliver the country from chaos. Stories had begun to surface about his captivity in Siberia. Other reports claimed that he was in China and even Vietnam. The clamour for information on Netaji's fate grew with time and unable to contain them, Indira Gandhi set up another commission in 1970—under Justice Gopal Das Khosla, former Chief Justice of the Punjab High Court—to enquire into the circumstances of Netaji's disappearance. The single member Khosla Commission was biased and ignored many important pieces of evidence that was submitted to it. This included a testimony by Shyam Lal Jain, a stenographer of Congress leader Asaf Ali who testified that in 1945 Jawaharlal Nehru had dictated a letter to him addressed to British Prime Minister Clement Atlee, informing that 'your war criminal'— Subhas Bose—had taken refuge in the Soviet Union. The diplomat and former parliamentarian Satya Narayan Sinha also testified that he had come across information that Netaji could have been locked up in Siberia and that he had informed Nehru of this. Nehru had dismissed him while Sarvepalli Radhakrishnan, who was India's ambassador to the Soviet Union from 1949 to 1952, had asked him to keep his own counsel. Needless to add—and possibly just as it was planned—the Khosla Commission came to the conclusion that Bose had indeed died in the air crash at Taipei.

But the saga of Netaji did not end here. When the Soviet Union began to break up in the early 1990s, hopes arose that secrets buried deep behind the Iron Curtain would finally see the light of day. In the three decades over which the Indo–Soviet friendship and partnership had been forged and nourished, the script remained officially dictated from both Soviet and Indian sides. There was no mention of the role of Subhas Bose in the history of relations between the two countries and certainly there was no acknowledgement that the entire cooperation had been forged by ignoring his existence and denying that he had ever lived in the Soviet Union. Now the script was expected to be written independently.

Glasnost and Perestroika led to the dissolution of the Soviet Union as it broke up into Russia and other successor states. But the same openness did not pervade the corridors of India's external affairs ministry. They continued to sing the same old tune. It was as if investigating Netaji in Russia was tantamount to destabilizing the bedrock of the Indo–Soviet relationship and would adversely impact 'national interest'. Nobody knew what this national interest entailed except that it was about the establishment's resolve to maintain the status quo. The documents regarding Netaji are, in all probability, hidden in archives in Russia or one of the former Soviet republics. Naturally the Government of India does not want to ferret out the truth by doing what is required. A little way forward has been made by independent Russian researchers but their interest in Netaji is limited. The Russian archives are not open to Indians. Moreover there are few Indian researchers who have a good grasp of the Russian language.

A team of researchers from the Asiatic Society of Kolkata did visit the Soviet Union in the mid-1990s and came across evidence that would suggest that Bose was present in the Soviet Union after the end of World War II. The team had however gone to research Indo–Soviet relations and was not looking into the whereabouts of Netaji.

A significant step forward was also taken by the Mukherjee Commission. Although the Commission's operation was hampered by an uncooperative Indian government which refused to declassify files on Netaji in its custody, it was able to establish that Bose did not die in the air crash. The reason: there had been no air crash in the first place. This was the first time that the official version purveyed since the early 1950s was sought to be proved wrong. The Commission also found that the ashes at Renkoji Temple were that of a dead Japanese soldier who had died a natural death in Taiwan the day the air crash was supposed to have taken place. The Commission's report submitted in 2005 was rejected by the United Progressive Alliance government in power at the Centre.

Official enquiries may have ceased or dried up but public investigation by spirited Indians continues to this day. There was now a new twist in the tale—was the *sannyasi* (monk), Gumnami Baba, the Indian leader in disguise? The holy man—who lived in the Uttar Pradesh town of Faizabad, the twin city of Ayodhya—was equally at ease speaking in English, Hindi and Bangla but was secretive, limited his interaction with a chosen few, and remained confined behind a curtain. When he died in September 1985 his quarters were searched by a few local citizens who were astonished by the items they found there. These included photographs of Netaji's parents that hung on the wall behind Gumnami Baba's bed, a copy of the *Gulag Archipelago* by Alexander Solzhenitsyn and numerous books on contemporary Indian politics. There were also a pile of newspapers from 1964–65 onwards, many of which had been annotated, among them Suresh Chandra Bose's *Dissentient Report* and literature pertaining to Netaji's life. The material was later locked up in the Faizabad treasury by the government. No proper inventory has been made of the records till date. The Mukherjee Commission probing the leads on Gumnami Baba visited Faizabad and took samples of handwriting of the holy man to compare it with that of Subhas Bose. One top handwriting expert said that indeed it was the same but two others did not confirm in the affirmative. A DNA test of old teeth in a match box in Baba's possession however did not match with samples taken from some of Subhas Bose's relatives. This anomaly apart, the match between Gumnami Baba and Subhas Bose seems to be close and thus the possibility of the holy man being the patriot in disguise cannot be ruled out. Justice M.K. Mukherjee was also caught on television saying that the Baba was in fact Bose. This was an off-record comment that was captured by mistake.

With the Uttar Pradesh government now allocating a separate budget to set up a museum to house Gumnami Baba's collections—after the Lucknow bench of the Allahabad High Court passed an order in January 2013—hopes have soared that the mystery of the holy man's origin will be solved to conclusively prove whether or not he was Subhas Chandra Bose. The seekers of truth hope that the collections of Gumnami Baba will throw up a memoir or a travelogue that would assist attempts to trace his life journey. It is believed that Baba has also left behind a map outlining the path he travelled from Siberia to north India that could go a long way in lifting the veil over Bose's last years.

Many who have come across the story of Gumnami Baba wonder how an intensely action-oriented man like Subhas Bose could have transformed into a reclusive mendicant. There are no easy answers. If the two were the same person, then the devastating experience in Siberia may have transformed Bose into someone totally different from his original persona. If an almost unknown episode from Bose's life is anything to go by, he must have been an intensely spiritual man. Apparently, his escape from house arrest in Calcutta was delayed because he waited for a *jaba* (hibiscus) flower from the famous shrine of Ma Kali on the banks of the Hooghly near Calcutta. Subhas dispatched his niece Ila for the purpose and once the flower arrived he touched it on his forehead and chest and put it in a pocket before leaving.

History is written from the point of view of the victor. The British won World War II and the Congress party came to power after India won freedom. The history of the freedom struggle that is propagated in India seeks to give credit only to the Congress party for winning freedom. But this is an imperfect story of how India became independent. There were many forces at play. A special effort seems to have been made in the early years after Independence to downplay the contribution made by Netaji and others in the struggle to attain freedom.

With the passage of time, however, the real contribution of Subhas Chandra Bose and the INA in the freedom movement is coming to light. The history of the INA and the Azad Hind government is not fully documented. As the Azad Hind government-in-exile was dissolved after the War most of its records were lost. Thus there is no authoritative account of the functioning of the Azad Hind government except for the memoirs and first-hand accounts left by survivors. However the exploits of the INA, which was raised by Bose from the ranks of prisoners of wars of the British Indian Army captured by the Japanese in places like Malaya, fired the imagination of the people of India. Although they ultimately lost to the superior strength and logistics of the British Army, the image of INA men seeking to invade India through the north-east in the first armed effort after the Revolt of 1857 stirred the emotions of millions. After the end of the War, which led to enormous losses of both life and property across the world, the British government realized that it did not have the wherewithal to hold on to the Indian Empire. The loyalty of the Indian Army to the British cause could not be taken for granted any more. British troops were not willing to wage a relentless battle far away from home. The INA had raised nationalist passions sky high and the mutinies by ratings of the Royal Indian Navy and men of the British Indian Army was an indicator of the shape of things to come. So in that sense the final blow to the British Empire was delivered by Netaji. The unprecedented surge of emotions witnessed at the trial of INA soldiers at the Red Fort demonstrated how the entire country idolised Netaji. But often such realisations come with the benefit of hindsight. It had not become clear to Bose himself that the end of the War had paved the way for Independence and that he had been instrumental in the whole exercise. He disappeared into the Soviet Union to fight a new battle for India's freedom not realizing that he had no need to hide anymore. Had he come to India he would have received a superhero's welcome and would have been unassailable. No British master or his Indian lackey would have dared touched him.

Subhas Bose's disappearance behind the Iron Curtain allowed the British to undertake a damage limitation exercise and withdraw from India before it became too late. They stirred the communal cauldron and appointed the vainglorious Earl of Mountbatten as the last Viceroy of India. The mischievous Mountbatten advanced the date of Independence by many months, announcing it less than two and a half months before the withdrawal of the British on 15 August. On the day of Partition, many did not know whether their villages and sub-divisions were in India or in Pakistan. Mountbatten was able to convince the ageing leaders of the Congress to agree to Partition sparking off the largest migration in human history besides leaving hundreds of thousands dead. Worse still, it left India with a permanent legacy of communal tensions and an enemy on the western border of the country.

A close follower of Gumnami Baba found him in a sombre mood one day and asked him whether he was angry. The Baba replied in Bangla:*'Jaar bhai thekey bhai neyi, Ma thekey Ma neyi, Desh thekey desh neyi, jaar adhikar neyi. Taar ki rag hotey parey? Taar sudhu hotey parey abhiman.'* ('Can a man who does not have brothers in spite of having them, who does not have a mother in spite of having her, who does not have a country or any rights, can such a person be angry? He can only have a deep sense of hurt.') If indeed Baba was Netaji, this was the state to which he had been reduced by the country for whose freedom he had so earnestly fought.

1

The Air Crash Story

On 15 August 1945, Japan surrendered to Allied forces, effectively marking the end of World War II. Germany had surrendered unconditionally around three months earlier—on 8 May. Netaji was then based in Singapore as the head of the Provisional Government of Azad Hind. When he heard the news, he knew that his hour of reckoning had arrived. The choice was between the devil and the deep blue sea. Netaji, as usual, kept a brave face. In a message to Indians in East Asia he said, 'a glorious chapter in India's struggle for freedom has come to an end but there is no power on earth that can keep India enslaved, India shall be free and before long.' To his soldiers in the Indian National Army (INA) he exhorted, 'the roads to Delhi are many and Delhi still remains our goal.' In his mind he knew that finding another road to Delhi was easier said than done.

Netaji called for a Cabinet meeting the same night. After deep confabulations it was decided that Netaji and the Cabinet would have to evacuate from Malaya immediately to avoid falling into the hands of the British forces. Located at the tip of the Malay peninsula, Singapore was being frequently bombed by the US Air Force and the Royal Navy was preparing to capture it. The Japanese had themselves told Netaji to move out to Saigon (now Ho Chi Minh City) before it was too late and even the INA chief of staff, Lieutenant Colonel Jagannathrao Krishnarao Bhonsle had proffered similar advice.

Netaji's choice was to get onto Russian held territory, if not Russia itself. This was a country that held a special place in Bose's heart. When he escaped from Calcutta in January 1941, Russia had been his preferred destination. When he could not contact the higher authorities in Moscow, he made his way to Berlin. At this point it appears that he felt that there were no other options left.

Netaji had been trying to establish contact with the Russians even before the Japanese had surrendered. He had dispatched his minister Anand Mohan Sahay to Tokyo in 1944 to meet with the Soviet ambassador to Japan, Jacob Malik (who was still continuing in his post because war between Japan and the Soviet Union was yet to be declared) and open a channel of communication with him. The meeting did not take place because the Japanese foreign minister Mamoru Shigemitsu dissuaded Sahay. A year later, in May 1945, Sahay wrote to Shigemitsu again to try to facilitate a meeting with Malik, but to no avail.

That Subhas Bose held great hopes regarding the Soviet Union is also clear from his radio speech to Indians from Bangkok on 14 June 1945. He said: 'Since the fall of Germany, Soviet Russia has become more outspoken about her plans of post-War reconstruction and she has made a number of moves on the Asiatic chessboard which have been exceedingly irritating to the Anglo–American powers. At the San Francisco Conference the Soviet foreign minister challenged the credentials of the representatives of India and the Philippines who were puppets of Britain and the United States, and he openly talked of a Free India and Free Philippines.' This was the United Nations Conference on International Organization held between April and late June 1945 which led to the establishment of the United Nations Charter. India, though still under British suzerainty, had a representation in the conference.

'It will be an adventure into the unknown,' Netaji told his Cabinet colleagues that night, his mind going back three months, to the day he heard of the German surrender. At that time Bose was on the outskirts of Bangkok and upon hearing the news went into a self-imposed retreat for a week to contemplate his next course of action. Having more or less decided that he would go over to the Russians, Netaji returned to Singapore. The day after the announcement of the Japanese surrender, Netaji informed the Japanese of his plans and asked them for assistance in travelling to Russian-held territory. There was consternation amongst the Japanese—with many feeling that he was about to forsake them after having obtained their full cooperation. There were others who felt that Bose's entry into Russia could work to Japanese advantage. After all, Russo–Japanese relations had been maintained on an even keel till the Russians declared war on Japan on 8 August 1945, a day after the first atomic bomb had been dropped on Hiroshima. After the nuclear bomb attack that sealed the fate of Japan, some top leaders of the country were planning to lobby the Soviet supremo Joseph Stalin to secure favourable terms of negotiations for their country. Moreover, after the two atomic bombs decimated millions, the Japanese were now wary of the United States. The Japanese had immense faith in Bose, who they thought was an 'Indian samurai' who might soften the Russians in their favour. After the end of the War, a Japanese interpreter, whose offices were used for meetings between Netaji and Japanese officials was interrogated by the Intelligence Bureau (IB) in November 1945. His narration (the record of which was declassified by India's Ministry of Defence in 1997) quotes Subhas Bose as telling the Japanese: 'In order to destroy a common enemy, Britain, both Japan and the Provisional Government should try every possible move and help each other. Therefore I earnestly request Tokyo to act as "go-between" and let me approach Soviet Russia. I have perfect confidence in my success in persuading Russia to help our Independence movement and at the same time I am sure I can do something to improve relations between Japan and Russia.'

In the end the Imperial General Headquarters (IGHQ) in Tokyo refused to accede to Bose's request. However, one person did. Field

Marshal Hisaichi Teruachi, commander of the Japanese forces in South-east Asia who was stationed in Saigon, decided to help the Indian revolutionary. Teruachi could afford to take his own decisions because he controlled a crucial part of the Japanese army and his cooperation would be needed to get his men to surrender. The Field Marshal—a wizened old aristocrat approaching seventy—had been closely associated with Netaji for two years and was sympathetic to him. He organized a plan for Netaji that would take the latter to Dairen in China. Here Bose would surrender to the advancing Soviet army and try his luck. Teruachi himself would give himself up to the Supreme Allied Commander South-east Asia, Lord Louis Mountbatten two months later. This was after the formal document confirming the surrender of Japanese forces was signed on 2 September on the deck of the USS *Missouri*. Soon after, he died as a prisoner of war.

The plane that would carry Subhas Bose and other members of his Cabinet would not be able to fly straight to Dairen. The flight was not meant specifically for Bose: it would be a regular military flight from Saigon flying to Tokyo via Dairen. In 1945, it was the capital of the Kwantung (Guandong) province, and the main centre of Japanese-controlled Manchuria. When Netaji decided to fly into Dairen it was still under Japanese control, but the Soviet army was expected to take over in a matter of days.

It is noteworthy that Emperor Hirohito did not use the Japanese equivalent of the word 'surrender' while declaring his country's capitulation, leading to a lot of confusion amongst his countrymen. In fact the Emperor had merely said that Japan would abide by the Potsdam Agreement. The heads of government of the United States, the Soviet Union and Great Britain had met in Potsdam on 17 July to decide on the penalties to be imposed on Germany (and other defeated countries like Japan). After Germany's unconditional surrender on 8 May, the country was broken into two parts. Japan held on but after the Emperor's statement, it was now apparent that the country was also ready for the punishment and other arrangements decided by the victors. This imperfect reading of the statement by the Japanese people and sections of the armed forces was the reason why Japanese military aircraft were still flying. The Emperor had effectively agreed to the surrender to buy protection from the Allies: he was under severe threat of a coup by members of his government, who wanted the War to continue and pointed out that Japan had never yet lost a war. Thus there was a divide in Japanese opinion.

While trying to contact the Soviet ambassador in Tokyo a year earlier, Bose must have been trying to assess the state of the Japanese in Manchuria—it is probable that he was ready for direct contact with the Russians if the Tokyo route failed and Japanese cooperation was not forthcoming. Netaji would have been assessing whether the optimism of sections of the Japanese establishment at keeping the Soviets at bay was supported by ground-level preparedness.

From Singapore, Netaji flew to Bangkok, where he deplaned for a few hours to confer with members of the Indian community, who had great hopes of his success. After that he reached Saigon. A Mitsubishi Ki-21 heavy bomber was waiting at Saigon to fly to Tokyo. A place was found for Bose in the plane. The other occupants were a group of Japanese army men and a crew of about five people. Although Netaji had many members of the INA with him, such as his secretary Lieutenant Colonel Habibur Rahman Khan, member of his Cabinet, Subbier Appadurai Ayer and Abid Hasan Safrani (Netaji's personal secretary and interpreter in Germany), there was only one vacant seat. Another seat was soon found for Rahman, Netaji's most trusted aide. The remaining members of the team remained in Saigon with the understanding that they would be accommodated in later flights to Tokyo. Among the Japanese on the flight was Lieutenant General Tsunamasa Shidei, Vice-Chief of the Japanese Kwantung Army in Manchuria. Netaji and Shidei were to deplane at Dairen and the Japanese general would negotiate and facilitate the INA chiefs surrender to the Soviet forces. Shidei was earlier the commander of Japanese forces in Burma but had been deployed to Manchuria just to facilitate Netaji's surrender before the

Russians. Shidei had been included in the plan at the insistence of Field Marshal Teruachi, since he was fluent in English, Japanese and Russian. He was also deeply knowledgeable about international war procedures, including the norms of surrender.

By all accounts the bomber was overloaded and later in the evening it stopped at a place called Tourane in Vietnam. It seems that during the stop-over, Bose confabulated with Habibur Rahman, making him swear that he would propagate the false story of an air crash. Rahman was never to let out the truth, even under the most severe pressure. The story to be disseminated was that the plane had crashed because it was carrying trunks with gold bars and other valuables that Indians in Saigon had handed over to Netaji towards the INA's efforts for India's independence. How would Rahman live to tell the tale? It would be said that the aircraft had crashed at a low height, as a result of which Rahman escaped without any injuries but Bose succumbed to third degree burns. Lieutenant General Shidei was also included in the plan.

As planned, the plane carrying Netaji touched down at Taihoku (Taipei) in Formosa (Taiwan) at midday on 18 August. After lunch and the offloading of some materials from the plane, the bomber took off at 2 pm, on its way to Tokyo. From here the air crash story kicked in. Within minutes, the plane had crashed, even as it was taking off. Netaji was admitted to the Nanmon Military Hospital and in spite of blood transfusions and the best efforts of doctors died within a couple of hours. Even though he had third degree burns, Bose was remarkably clear in his mind and told Rahman to continue the fight for India's freedom. The next day he was cremated. Two days later his ashes were carried to Tokyo in an urn by the Japanese and handed over to the representative of the Indian Independence League in that city. After a memorial service, the urn was handed over to the Buddhist Renkoji Temple in Tokyo in mid-September. The news about Bose's death was announced on 23 August by Domei, a Japanese news agency (forerunner of the present-day Kyodo News). According to the air crash story that has been handed down the years, it was not just Netaji who perished that 'fateful' afternoon. The General's death was also announced along with that of Bose by Domei. Since he was the man who was to make Bose's surrender to the Russians possible, a cover was needed for him, and what better cover for both than to have died in the crash?

Although Subhas Bose was a stickler for details, there were some holes in his plot. According to the story, Netaji sustained burns as he was running out of the aircraft while it was on fire. Habibur Rahman also ran out of the plane, through the same fire, without any injuries. There are no pictures of an injured Bose in the hospital or for that matter any images of his mortal remains. Many years later, due to the intrepid efforts of an Indian journalist and Right To Information activist Anuj Dhar—who has researched in depth on the circumstances of Bose's disappearance—it is now known that no plane crash took place at Taihoku airport during that period.

In response to a specific query from Dhar in 2005 the Minister for Transportation and Communication of Taiwan, Lin Lung Som, wrote back, 'During the period 14 August to 25 October 1945 no evidence shows that one plane had ever crashed at the old Matsuyana airport (now Taipei domestic airport) carrying Subhas Chandra Bose.' The genuineness of the email was verified by Justice Manoj Kumar Mukherjee, the retired judge of the Supreme Court appointed by the Government of India in 1999 to unravel the mystery of the disappearance of Netaji. The Commission too rejected the air crash theory having found out that the only air crash that had taken place in Taiwan was on 20 September 1945, that of an US Air Force transportation plane carrying released American prisoners of war. This air crash was logged 200 nautical miles away from Taipei. The Mukherjee Commission also noted that the register of cremation of Taipei for the period 17–27 August 1945 did not record the names Subhas Chandra Bose and Lieutenant General Shidei. Neither did it contain the names of the pilots who were supposed to have perished in the same crash. There were no reports in the newspapers of the crash the following day. The Commission concluded that the ashes kept in the urn at Renkoji Temple were that of a Japanese soldier, Ichiro Okura who had died from cardiac arrest.

An earlier committee as also a commission of inquiry on Netaji's disappearance stood by the air crash theory. These were set up since from the very first day, news of Netaji's death in an air crash was treated with disbelief in India and amongst foreign intelligence agencies. People believed that given Netaji's penchant for secrecy and use of aliases, this was the sort of story that he would fabricate so as to escape unnoticed and continue his mission. His legendary submarine journey from Germany to Asia and the fact that he escaped from India, throwing dust in the eyes of the British Indian police, had led to the belief that Bose was capable of any feat.

In 1956 a three-member committee was set up under Shah Nawaz Khan to probe Netaji's disappearance. Khan had been a member of the INA and was arraigned by the British in the Red Fort INA trials after the end of the War. He was to become a Member of Parliament and lost much of the fire that propelled him in the INA days. In other words, he had become an establishment man and would seem inclined to do whatever was wanted of him. The other members of the Committee were an Indian Civil Service (ICS) officer S.N. Maitra (who had been nominated by the West Bengal government) and Suresh Chandra Bose. The Committee examined witnesses in India, Thailand, Vietnam and Japan and came to the conclusion by majority opinion that Netaji had died in the air crash.

Suresh Chandra Bose did not agree to this conclusion and wrote and independently published the *Dissentient Report* which pointed out that crucial evidence was kept away from him and that the Committee had failed to acknowledge the conflicting testimonies of many witnesses. He also hinted that efforts were made to force him to sign the Committee's report. Significantly in his dissent note, Suresh Chandra Bose pointed out that Lieutenant General Harukai Isayama, Japanese Chief of Staff in Formosa (Taiwan) with headquarters at Taihoku (who was therefore expected to know everything about the air crash) had testified before the Committee that he heard about the death of Netaji and Lieutenant General Shidei in the air crash only when he went to the office the next day. Stating that Shidei was his friend and former classmate, he said that he heard of the accident from his staff officer. It is strange that the General had been informed of his classmate and fellow officer's sudden death a day later. Needless to say, the dissent note robbed the authenticity of the Shah Nawaz Committee report and made the former INA officer's intentions appear suspicious. The Committee's blatantly fixed report also had the impact of whetting public appetite for correct information about Netaji's death: people wanted to know why the Indian government was trying hard to prove that Netaji had perished in the air crash. More of this is detailed in a later chapter.

The demand for a proper inquiry into the whereabouts of Netaji persisted and by 1970 the chorus had grown louder. In 1970, the Indira Gandhi government set up a one-man inquiry commission to find some answers. Justice Gopal Das Khosla, a retired Chief Justice of the Punjab High Court was entrusted with the task. Justice Khosla was engaged with many other activities and was able to complete his report only four years later, concluding that Netaji had died in the air crash, ignoring crucial pieces of evidence. He went out of his way to discredit theories that suggested that Netaji was alive and questioned the motives of those who asserted that he did not die in the air crash, suggesting that they were driven by political considerations or were just seeking attention.

The British had carried out their own investigations. Within a year of the alleged air crash, the British asked a political intelligence official Lieutenant Colonel John Figgess to investigate the matter. After speaking extensively to witnesses, including those at the hospital, Figgess concluded that a 'certain S.C. Bose had died on August 18, 1945 at the hospital' at Taipei as a result of heart failure due to multiple burns and shocks. In his report on 19 July 1946, Figgess asserted that the possibility of witness accounts being fabricated 'must be excluded'. Figgess' report was obviously not fixed; the intelligence official was really making efforts to find out the truth. But if he was fooled into believing that Bose had perished this would mean that there was a pre-arranged Japanese collusion to tutor witnesses and agree on a consistent story. This would also imply that the Japanese collusion extended not only to the level of the regional Field Marshal but also included the IGHQ which had, as earlier stated in this chapter, rejected Bose's plan to go to the Soviet Union. The denial to assist Bose had been possibly only for the record and elements in the Japanese establishment still impressed with the 'Indian samurai' were willing to assist him in the hope that he would also get a better deal for Japan. Either way, Japan had surrendered and there was nothing to be lost by pushing Netaji into Russia. Whatever the authenticity of the Figgess report, its conclusion convinced a section of Netaji's family that he had indeed perished in the air crash.

Yet the British had not been too sure. An IB communication in February 1946 from intelligence officers W. McKWright and Major Countenay Young (quoted in Suresh Bose's dissent note) states: 'We have at last completed an examination of the information available relating to the alleged death of Bose and the result is not entirely satisfactory for it reveals many discrepancies, which until clarified, make any definitive conclusion on the incident a little doubtful.'

2

Surrendering to the Russians

Netaji's Japanese-mediated surrender to the Russians was not a sound idea. Subhas Chandra Bose knew that he was taking a chance. Apparently he told his colleagues that he was prepared for any consequences, including imprisonment and death. However, Netaji also glossed over some flaws in his own plans.

For one, relations between Japan and Russia were strained and a leader from the losing side who had capitulated—Netaji was aligned with the Axis powers which lost to the Allied forces—would have had limited bargaining power. He would be seen as an extension of the Japanese side, which was now being penalized for participating in World War II. In an act that would hasten the end of the War in Asia, the Soviet Union unilaterally breached the treaty of neutrality, two years after a brief border war in 1939. The treaty signed in 1941 had stipulated that the two countries would desist from hostilities against each other in the midst of the World War.

But behind Japan's back—in February 1945, as the War was winding down—Soviet leader Joseph Stalin acceded to US President Franklin D. Roosevelt's suggestion at the Yalta Conference that his country would begin hostilities against Japan within ninety days of the defeat of Germany. Accordingly the Soviets began invading Japanese-controlled Manchuria on 8 August 1945—just two days after the United States dropped the atomic bomb on Hiroshima. Some 1.6 million Soviet troops were involved in the massive operation, which many historians now believe was the primary reason behind the Japanese capitulation (and not the nuclear attack). About 84,000 Japanese soldiers and 12,000 Soviet troops perished with the Red Army just 50 km from the northern island of Hokkaido as hostilities drew to a close.

The Japanese–Soviet conflict dated back to the Czarist period and was rooted in a desire for dominance of north-east Asia by both the Russian and Japanese empires. There was a war between the two nations over the oil-rich southern Sakhalin and Kuril islands in 1904–05 but the Russians wrested back the territory from Japan at the end of World War II. There are still differences between the two countries regarding the islands. The two countries clashed again militarily at the end of World War I when Japan sent out troops to counter the Bolshevik presence in the Russian Civil War. The Bolshevik party led by Vladimir Lenin had seized control of the Russian countryside and several government ministries in October 1917. The Treaty of Brest–Litovsk between Russia and Germany in March 1918 ended Russian participation in World War I seven months before the War ended in November 1918. The entry of the Bolsheviks set off the Russian Civil War, where 'Reds' were ranged against the anti-socialist 'Whites' as well as non-Bolshevik socialists. Between 1918 and 1922, 70,000 Japanese troops occupied Vladivostok, seven time-zones away from Moscow in Russia's Far East. During World War I, Japan was aligned with the Entente Powers or Allies, which included the Russians. Japan was propelled in its actions by the European countries to counter the rise of Communism in the Soviet Union, by restricting it in Far East Asia.

The scenario changed in the run up to World War II. On 19 September 1931, Japan began its invasion of Manchuria—a huge territory—and set up the puppet state of Manchukuo. The deposed Qing emperor Puyi was made the nominal ruler. The infant Puyi had been the last emperor of China when his regime was overthrown and the Republic of China created in 1912. The Japanese administered the territory with a heavy hand. They did not exactly endear themselves to the local populace of Manchuria, both Russian and Chinese.

With Manchuria under their control, Japan began wars with the Soviet Union on the Manchuria–Mongolia border. The relations between the two countries deteriorated sharply after 1936 when Japan and Nazi Germany signed the anti-Communist Anti-Comintern Pact. A series of border skirmishes from 1935 onwards led to the defeat of the Japanese in 1939 at the Battle of Khalkin Gol, on the border between Mongolia and Manchuria. The Soviets believed that this loss had led Japan to sign the neutrality treaty in 1941. In fact, after Germany attacked the Soviet Union later that year (breaking the non-aggression pact that the two countries had entered in 1939) Japan had also considered attacking the Russians. The Soviets therefore had an abiding distrust of the Japanese and this was not something that stacked in favour of Netaji Subhas Chandra Bose, as he gave up to the Soviet forces outside Dairen, sometime on 18 or 19 August 1945.

The trail goes cold here. The circumstances of the surrender and what happened to Netaji in the immediate aftermath can only be recreated with the limited information available in the public domain. Netaji's flight reached Dairen in the afternoon of a particular day in August 1945. After disembarking, Subhas Bose ate a modest meal of a banana and some tea. Thereafter accompanied by Lieutenant General Tsunamasa Shidei and two of his Japanese aides, Netaji started off in a jeep towards the point at which the Russian troops were garrisoned. After about three hours, the driver of the jeep came back and gave the green signal to the pilot of the flight from Saigon to proceed to Tokyo. This vital information comes from a very strange source. Shyam Lal Jain was a stenographer with Congress leader Asaf Ali in New Delhi. In his deposition before the Justice G.D. Khosla Commission in 1970, Jain said that he was summoned to the residence of Asaf Ali on either 26 or 27 December 1945 by Jawaharlal Nehru (who was then only a Congress leader) and given a letter to type that had an indistinct signature at the bottom. The letter read, 'Netaji reached Dairen in Manchuria at

1-30 p.m. on 23 August 1945 by plane from Saigon. He had plenty of gold with him in bars and ornaments.' The letter went on to recount how along with Shidei, Netaji hopped onto a jeep and drove towards Russian territory. After this Nehru asked Jain to type another letter, this time addressed to Clement Atlee, who had taken over as Great Britain's prime minister after Winston Churchill lost to the Labour Party in the 1945 general elections in the United Kingdom. The letter said, 'Dear Mr Atlee: I understand from a most reliable source that Subhas Chandra Bose, your war criminal, has been allowed to enter Russian territory by Stalin. This is clear treachery and betrayal of faith by the Russians, as they were allies of the British-Americans. Please take care and do what you consider proper and fit.' This damning piece of evidence was not acknowledged by the Khosla Commission, which perhaps had its own reason to doubt the authenticity of the testimony. Perhaps the Commission felt that the testimony of a stenographer could not be taken so seriously.

The letter to Attlee also raises another question. Did Netaji reach Dairen on 23 August and not on 18 or 19 August, as was believed and that he flew in from Saigon. Does this imply that Bose was holed up in Saigon, plotting his disappearance along with his Japanese colleagues and instructing colleagues like Habibur Rahman about what to tell the world? Or, alternatively, is it that Netaji took the same route to Dairen from Saigon via Tourane and Taipei? However, the journey was undertaken on 23 August and not on 18 August, as the story from the Japanese news agency announcing 'Netaji's death' suggests. It is still uncertain.

That Netaji was trying to go to Dairen was alluded to even by the Shah Nawaz Committee. It quoted the testimony of Major General Saburo Isoda, the head of the Hikari Kikan, an organization that liaised between the Japanese government and the INA saying that Netaji had decided to proceed to Tokyo via Saigon and from there to Dairen. The Committee said that it was a coincidence that Netaji was travelling in the same plane as Lieutenant General Shidei and 'it appears fell with the idea that he should go up to Dairen with General Shidei.'

One can only surmise on the chain of events after Bose's surrender. Whatever the date, the Russians must have been very surprised to obtain Bose's surrender. The Indian leader must have been taken in protective custody even as information passed up the Soviet government communication channels for instructions from higher authorities. After a few days, Netaji would have been moved to more secure premises. Since Siberia was close by, Bose would probably have been taken to a top internal security jail. Or was he taken to Moscow? It would have been in Bose's own interest to go to Omsk in Siberia, where he had sent an agent earlier to establish an office of the Provisional Government of Azad Hind.

As it turned out, there would be no final instructions from the higher authorities about what to do with Bose. He may have been an extremely important person in India, but abroad he was of limited value. Moreover, in the busy closing days of World War II, it is not even clear how much attention the Netaji affair received at the hand of the Soviets. Lieutenant General Shidei's fate remained unclear even as his service book showed that he had died in war on 18 August 1945 (this was discovered by Suresh Chandra Bose). This implies that he had not come back after facilitating Netaji's surrender, otherwise he would have been registered as having surrendered before the Allied forces. In all probability the Japanese general remained in Russia along with Subhas Bose.

One thing is certain. The Soviets would have wanted to keep Netaji incarcerated in secrecy and not allow other Allied powers to know that they held him. After all, in the world of international diplomacy, information is power and is often shared only on a need to know basis. The Allied forces might have fought together against the common enemy—the Nazis—but had differences within themselves. In fact, the beginnings of the Cold War that continued for forty years could be discerned soon after the end of World War II.

It was not that Nehru's letter to Atlee was the first to alert the British that Netaji was in Soviet custody. On 25 October 1945 a note from the

British Indian government came to the British Cabinet and the latter approved that 'Russia may accept Bose under special circumstances. If this is the case we should not demand him back.' Prime Minister Atlee is reported to have said, 'Let him remain where he is.' The British had been mulling over the best way to tackle Netaji and INA members from 15 August 1945—the day Japan announced its decision to surrender. Within eight days—coincidentally the day that the 'death of Netaji' was announced—Sir R.F. Mudie, home member of the Viceroy, Lord Archibald Wavell's Executive Council, had moved a file on how to deal with the matter. Was Subhas Bose to be arrested and tried? If he had to be tried should that be in India or abroad? Among the options considered was a trial by military court either in Burma, Malaya or India for waging war against the King Emperor or to intern him in India or some other British possession like Seychelles. On gauging the public mood, Mudie had figured out that it would not be easy to interrogate Bose and bring him to trial in India because of his high stature in the country. In fact an attempt to do this was bound to backfire. Thus the decision of the British government not to fuss over the location of Bose was a practical way of dealing with the delicate situation and keeping the popular Indian leader away from the public eye.

The British, who lorded over many parts of India, could not lay their hands on Netaji. However, neither were they willing to let their empire collapse. To send out the message that they were still in command, the colonial masters held a public trial of the captured INA soldiers, between November 1945 and May 1946. The first three INA members to be put up for the public court martial had formerly been officers of the British Indian Army: Lieutenant Colonel Shah Nawaz Khan, Colonel Prem Kumar Sahgal and Colonel Gurbaksh Singh Dhillon. These officers had been captured as prisoners of war by the Japanese in Malaya, Singapore and Burma respectively. They were inducted into the INA by Netaji and fought as part of the INA alongside the Japanese. They were charged by the British with 'waging war against the King-Emperor.' Incidentally Shah Nawaz Khan had played a prominent part in the Imphal campaign of the INA and had come out with flying colours.

The groundswell of opposition against the trial was unprecedented and had not been anticipated by the British. There was a huge public outcry and hundreds of meetings were organized across the country to express gratitude to the INA men. The main political parties, Congress and the Muslim League, made a huge political issue out of the trials. The Congress set up a defence committee under Bhulabhai Desai, Tej Bahadur Sapru, Kailash Nath Katju, Jawaharlal Nehru and Asaf Ali to appear for the accused. Even though the conservative sections of the press asked for clemency for what they termed as the misguided men, soon a campaign began, supporting 'patriots, not traitors'. The British had expected the loyalty of the Indian forces that had fought on their behalf but soon realized that even this was doubtful and the ranks of such forces could not be relied on. A huge naval mutiny broke out on 18 February 1946 in the ranks of the Royal Indian Navy—from Karachi to Bombay and Calcutta to Visakhapatnam—which shook the foundations of British rule over India. There was an army mutiny in the last week of February in Jubbulpore (Jabalpur) and to the foreign rulers it seemed that an encore of the rebellion of 1857 was imminent.

Khan, Sahgal and Dhillon were sentenced to transportation for life during the court martial but the punishment could not be carried out. Field Marshal Claude Auchinleck, the commander-in-chief of the British Indian Army, had to commute the sentences. A second court martial—that of Abdul Rashid, Shingara Singh, Fateh Khan and Captain Malik Munawar Khan Awan which commenced at the Red Fort had to be shifted out to an adjoining building. If the British had tried to revive memories of the historic trial of Bahadur Shah Zafar, the last Mughal emperor, ninety years earlier at the Red Fort, they probably realized that Indians could not be browbeaten anymore.

While all this was taking place, Netaji was waiting for Godot, probably in the confines of a Russian internal security prison.

Presumably, he would not have access to English newspapers or radio and so had scarce knowledge of what was happening in the world, let alone the INA trials. A man with a never-say-die attitude, he was, in all probability, seeking an appointment with Stalin. The meeting, he would have argued, would be to represent to the Russian leader the genuineness of the Indian cause and its desire to escape the clutches of colonial Britain. Free India, he would argue, would work hand-in-hand with the Soviet Union to set up a new world order. But the Indian leader probably did not receive any assistance within the prison. In his last months in South-east Asia, while contemplating the cross-over to the Soviet Union, Netaji was banking on the support of A.C.N. Nambiar, his deputy in Germany, a hardcore Communist who had spent many years in the Soviet Union and had great contacts there. After the surrender of Germany, Subhas Bose had expected Nambiar to lobby with the Kremlin on behalf of the Azad Hind government. However, Nambiar was arrested in June 1945 in Vienna and interrogated for his possible links with the Nazis and Bose's hopes were dashed.

In this same period, parallel trials of Japanese 'war criminals' were underway in Tokyo at the International Military Tribunal for the Far East. This was established by the US administration in January 1946 with the supreme commander of the Allied Forces General Douglas McArthur initiating arrests. The tribunal, which was nothing but a kangaroo court, had many members, including an Indian, Justice Radhabinod Pal. In the end, six defendants were sentenced to death by hanging in what was described as the 'victor's justice'. This included the former Japanese Prime Minister Hideki Tojo, the commander of the Japanese Burma Area Army, General Hietaro Kimura and General Kenji Doihara, chief of the intelligence services in Manchuria. Extraordinary efforts were made by the court to ensure that blame for the war-time atrocities was not attributed to Emperor Hirohito and his family members. They were not even tried. Although the Japanese forces had undoubtedly committed atrocities directed at the civilian population and prisoners of war, most of them who were sentenced were punished on less than perfect evidence and hearsay. In his dissent report, Justice Pal did not find any of the defendants guilty. In the end, the six awarded capital punishment were hanged on 23 December 1948 but since there was a fear that it would antagonize the Japanese people, the sentence was carried out in secrecy. The other indicted people—in fact all of them were found guilty—were sent to jail. Sixteen of them were sentenced for life.

Netaji had close ties with Tojo and other high-ranking Japanese ministers and generals. In fact after reaching Japan from Germany, Netaji had called on Prime Minister Tojo to discuss his plans. The two apparently hit it off though Tojo was initially reluctant to meet Bose and made him wait for three weeks. Once Tojo had met Netaji he was highly impressed and within days invited the latter to the Japanese Parliament (Diet). Tojo announced, 'Japan is firmly resolved to extend all means… to achieve Independence of India.' Incidentally when Emperor Hirohito declared that he was surrendering, Tojo had opposed the plan. The other generals who were sent to the gallows, Heitaro Kimura, Iwane Matsui and Kenji Doihara, were all known to Netaji and had worked closely with him. Kimura, the commander of the Japanese forces, had a tough time convincing Bose to withdraw the INA forces in Burma after fortune turned against them. Kimura started withdrawing in April 1945 after Burmese rebel forces put his forces under pressure, but it took three days to get Netaji on board.

From one point of view, the decision to surrender to the Russians was a sound idea, even though Netaji was lost to history. When the war ceased, the Japanese surrendered to the United States. Had Netaji remained in Singapore, Bangkok or Saigon he too would have been taken hostage by the Americans? It is conceivable, although not necessary, that Bose could have been tried along with the Japanese. This would have been disastrous he too may have been sentenced to death. Of course, going by the impact of the INA trials, it is doubtful whether the British could have risked sentencing him. The British had played the game of intrigue—as reported in the introduction to this book—and planted misleading information to sow doubts in the minds of the Soviets.

If the testimonies before the Shah Nawaz Committee can be taken as fact it would seem that Bose had also contemplated surrendering to the Americans. Surrendering to the British was certainly not part of his plan. Major General Isoda had told the Committee that if a move to Russian-held Manchuria proved difficult, Bose had thought of surrendering to the Americans in Tokyo. If that had happened, Netaji's fate would not have been shrouded in secrecy, there would have been no Iron Curtain blocking off the flow of information.

Safe in Russian custody, Netaji was largely forgotten until the Japanese ministers, generals and high officials who had been sentenced to death were hanged.

The Nuremberg trials had also begun by this time. Between 20 November 1945 and 1 October 1946 German war criminals were put under trial. Joachim von Ribbentrop, Hitler's foreign minister—with whom Subhas Bose had a good relationship—was sent to the gallows. Of course, the main culprits of Nazi Germany, Hitler, Himmler and Goebbels, had committed suicide many months before the trials started. Thus it was only at the end of 1948 that the Russians were free to take a decision on the future of Netaji. The question is, did they have the inclination?

3

Stalin, Nehru and Netaji

Joseph Stalin believed that the freedom of India was a ruse created by colonial powers that intended to exit India before the rising wave against them turned into a tide. The British would be replaced by Indians who represented the same interests—there would only be a change of power in the upper echelons and India would continue to be part of the British–American lobby. Stalin also had doubts about whether all the British occupiers would leave. Would armed forces in independent India be controlled by Indians or the British? Stalin's impression was that the elimination of foreign imperialism was inextricably linked to violent uprisings and the overthrow of feudal lords and the landed bureaucracy. Since the transfer of power in India did not involve a revolution, the freedom of India was a sham, a bourgeoisie conspiracy crafted by imperialists.

Stalin's views are reflected in a series of articles by analyst Valeriy Kashin published between May and June 2012 in the *Russia & India Report*, a publication promoted by the *Rossiyskaya Gazeta*, the official daily newspaper of the Russian government. In one of his articles, Kashin quotes the Russian Indologist, Grigory Kotovsky who said that Stalin thought Nehru was an agent of American imperialism and that the Soviet Union's foreign minister, Vyacheslav Molotov considered Nehru to be a British intelligence agent. His dislike for Indian leaders was so strong that Stalin did not even think it necessary to send his condolences after the assassination of Mahatma Gandhi, although India and the Soviet Union had established diplomatic relations after India became free.

Kirill Vasilyevich Novikov, the first Soviet ambassador to India, says that before leaving for India he was 'instructed by Comrade Stalin to remember that the Indian government came to power on 15 August 1947 as a result of the deal made between the Indian national bourgeoisie, feudal overlords and British imperialism.' Novikov submitted this in a report on 5 July 1949 to the foreign policy committee of the Communist Party of the Soviet Union. Once marked secret, it is now kept at the Russian State Archive of Socio-Political History.

These candid opinions of Stalin may not have been known to Netaji, although an assessment of contemporary events would have given him more than an inkling of the Soviet leader's views on India. Such a view would have encouraged Netaji to surrender to the Red Army. As long as Stalin had a rather dim view of India's new rulers, Bose stood a chance of getting assistance from the Soviet leader.

But political assessments change. Novikov himself did a lot to change the assessment of the Nehru government in the eyes of the regime back home. He reported back that the freedom of India should not be viewed as the 'political farce' that Stalin believed it to be. Despite the manner in which India had won Independence, it was not being run by the erstwhile British rulers. He also gave a favourable opinion of Nehru, pointing out that he was a leader of the liberation movement, a subtle politician and a smart parliamentarian who was adept at gauging the national mood of his country and enjoyed immense authority.

At the same time, the Nehru regime also tried to foster close relations with the Soviet Union. This may have to do with the United States' attempts to bring Pakistan under its sphere of influence. Moreover, after Nehru tried and failed to receive food aid during his visit to the United States, a request was made to the Soviet Union. The latter obliged.

In 1949, Nehru appointed the academician Sarvepalli Radhakrishnan, later to be President of India, as the Indian ambassador to the Soviet Union. Both Radhakrishnan and his successor—career diplomat K.P.S. Menon—made a huge effort to engage with Stalin's regime and successfully altered his views on India. Stalin was generally reluctant to meet foreign ambassadors but he received Radhakrishnan twice and K.P.S. Menon once. The French and Argentinian ambassadors were the only other national representatives to be granted an audience with Stalin. He also refused to meet India's first ambassador to the Soviet Union, Vijayalakshmi Pandit, who served from 1947 to 1949.

The details of Radhakrishnan's and Menon's meetings with Stalin, now available in the public domain, show the way they courted Stalin and how they were able to change his resistance to India.

The first meeting between Radhakrishnan and Stalin took place on 15 January 1950 at the Kremlin—just a few days before India was declared a Republic on 26 January.

In a secret telegram, CCB No. 397 sent to the secretary general of the foreign ministry, Ratan Kumar Nehru, the ambassador recorded that he had apprised Stalin that India's policy of neutrality was genuine and that India was anxious to avoid Cold War tactics and anti-Communist pacts. Nehru had in fact affirmed this, Radhakrishnan had added, to which Stalin nodded in approval.

In his conversation with the ambassador, Stalin said that he had been told that Nehru was visiting London—two days prior to this interaction—and had also wanted to visit Moscow, but changed his mind since he was unsure of the reception he would receive. Radhakrishnan told Stalin that he was unaware of this fact but that the Indian prime minister would be glad to visit Moscow anytime.

At his next meeting with Stalin on 5 April 1952, two years later, Radhakrishnan told Stalin that India was as much against capital exploitation as the Soviet Union and that the two shared the same economic objectives. In affirmation of the Indian position, Radhakrishnan said, 'We are passing through critical times. We have got rid of various forms of exploitation, we have rid ourselves of foreign domination and we have got rid of princely rule. We hope to tackle the problem of our landlords equally successfully.'

Stalin, who had been smoking heavily all through the meeting, said, 'It will be good if you succeed in doing it.' The Indian ambassador stated, 'We are not with America and we are not with any power. We act according to our sense of right and do not yield to political or economic pressure.'

Stalin had earlier told Radhakrishnan, 'The United States and Britain look down on Asian people as backward. We treat them as equals. It helps us to conduct a correct policy. The Americans and British treat them superciliously.'

From his interactions with India's ambassadors, it seems that Stalin's knowledge of India was rudimentary. He had asked Radhakrishnan—was Ceylon (now Sri Lanka) a part of India? At a meeting with Menon on 17 February 1953 he had wanted to know if the primary language of India was Hindi, Urdu or Gujarati.

Stalin also enquired about India's relations with Pakistan and whether the two countries were planning a federation. The ambassador replied that this was not possible citing the bitterness between Hindus and Muslims and briefed Stalin on the basis for the creation of Pakistan. 'How primitive it is, how absurd it is to create and run a state on the basis of religion,' Stalin commented. Echoing his predecessor, Menon explained Nehru's concept of a secular state and his unflinching adherence to that idea. He pointed out that the fifty-million Muslims in India were made to feel that they were equal partners with other communities in the country's destiny in every way. 'Of course they are Indians and your policy is the right one,' Stalin had said.

Stalin died on 3 March 1953—barely a fortnight after he met Menon. But it was clear that by the time he died he was convinced of the intentions of the post-Independence Indian establishment. There would be no need for Subhas Chandra Bose. For his labours, Radhakrishnan was awarded the highest Indian civilian honour, the Bharat Ratna in 1954 (in the first batch of three Indians to be so honoured) and was first made the Vice-President and then the President of India. Radhakrishnan's elevation had caused ripples in Congress circles and many leaders like Maulana Abul Kalam Azad obliquely hinted that there were better candidates. Radhakrishnan knighted by the British earlier and with no previous experience of politics and statesmanship had performed a yeoman's role for Nehru.

All the while that Stalin was being courted by Nehru's men, he was aware of Netaji's presence in a Soviet prison. Alexander Kolesnikov, a former Major-General of the Warsaw Pact countries who accessed the Russian military archives in Paddolsk (40 km outside Moscow) in October 1996 found papers which suggested that in October 1946 Stalin and his men were discussing how to deal with Bose. Kolesnikov's findings were presented before an Indian parliamentary delegation that visited the Russian Federation in 1996 and two members—Chitta Basu and Jayanta Roy of the All-India Forward Bloc (founded by Netaji in 1939) brought back the details to India. Subsequently these findings were presented through an affidavit before the Mukherjee Commission. The affidavit was filed by Professor Purabi Roy, a researcher investigating Netaji's case, who had visited Moscow and put Kolesnikov on the job. Roy accessed a 1946 report of a Soviet secret agent writing from Bombay, 'It is not possible to work with Nehru and Gandhi. We have to use Subhas Bose.' At the very least, this proves that Bose was alive in 1946.

Even Nehru and Radhakrishnan were aware of the possibility of Netaji's incarceration in a Soviet prison. Satya Narayan Sinha, who had served as an aide to Nehru and excelled in foreign languages, had deposed before the Khosla Commission in October 1970 that a former NKVD agent (NKVD was the precursor to the KGB) named Kuzlov had told him that Netaji was a prisoner in Cell Number 45 of Yakutsk Prison in Siberia. Kuzlov, suspected of being a Trotskyite, had been jailed in Yakutsk by the Stalin regime. He was later rehabilitated and provided Sinha with this information in 1954 in Moscow. Although the Khosla Commission had failed to acknowledge Sinha's testimony, it had questioned him closely. The Commission asked Sinha whether Kuzlov had mentioned the name of Netaji or had merely said that he had seen an important Indian leader. Sinha stood by his statement that Kuzlov had stated that he had met Netaji in Calcutta. In fact Kuzlov even knew the location of Bose's ancestral home in the eastern Indian city. Till 1934 Kuzlov was in charge of training Indians for his country's local intelligence operations.

Sinha also told the Commission that he had been making enquiries about Netaji since 1949 and had run into Karl Leonhard, a former German spy who had served time in Siberia after the Germans lost the war to the Soviet Union. Leonhard had told Sinha,'I have come to know that your leader Bose is also a prisoner.' On hearing this Sinha met Nehru on 13 April 1950 and apprised him of what he had learnt. Sinha told the Khosla Commission that Nehru had not shown much interest but said,'I will check up the matter, but I think this is American propaganda.' Sinha said that he again took up the matter with Nehru on 16 January 1951 on the sidelines of a meeting of ambassadors but to no effect. Sinha had also raised the matter with Radhakrishnan for whom he had worked as an interpreter in Geneva. According to Sinha's deposition, 'He (Radhakrishnan) told me not to meddle in these things. You will be spoiling your career.' Sinha had also met Georgy Mukherjee, son of Abani Mukherjee, an Indian Communist who had joined Stalin but later fell foul of him and was packed off to Siberia. Sinha said that Mukherjee had told him that Netaji had been imprisoned in a cell adjoining his father in Siberia. He had also added that Netaji went by the name Khilsai Malang there. However there is a little discrepancy in this part of the testimony because Abani Mukherjee was executed in a Stalinist purge in October 1937. Since Netaji was in the Soviet Union only after August 1945 he could not have encountered Abani Mukherjee.

Sensing opposition to his views from within the Indian establishment Sinha had desisted from deposing before the Shah Nawaz Committee in 1956. In this period his professional life also saw a transformation.

After two years (1950–52) with the Indian Foreign Service, he joined politics and was elected to the Lok Sabha from Bihar in 1952 as a member of the Indian National Congress, and went on to have a long career as a lawmaker. He seems to have been a man with a conscience and thus when called upon by the Khosla Commission in October 1970—he was nearly seventy then—Sinha deposed before it and said that he had been rebuked in 1954 by Nehru for bringing up the subject of Netaji's whereabouts. Sinha said that after an open debate in Parliament, Nehru had written to him enquiring after his frequent visits to the American embassy in Delhi and whether he was spying for them.

The Khosla Commission also ignored Sinha's revelations just as it failed to obtain the submissions from Sarvepalli Radhakrishnan who had by then retired as the President of India and was living in Madras (Chennai). Another witness had deposed that Radhakrishnan had actually met Subhas Chandra Bose in Moscow in 1948, visiting the Soviet capital in a non-official capacity, as a participant in a philosophy conference. This was S.M. Goswami, a retired special officer of the Anti-Corruption Bureau of the West Bengal government who said that Radhakrishnan had apprised him in 1954 about the 1948 meeting. Radhakrishnan had revealed that Netaji had requested him to arrange for his return to India. Goswami deposed that Radhakrishnan had told him that on his return to India he had spoken of his meeting with Netaji to 'higher ups' who did not want this information disclosed. Goswami had first met Radhakrishnan to present him a book, *Netaji Mystery Revealed* that he had written. Goswami also testified that he had again met Radhakrishnan in July 1962 when as President of India he was visiting Calcutta to attend the funeral of deceased West Bengal chief minister, Bidhan Chandra Roy. Radhakrishnan had reaffirmed that he had indeed met Netaji. The President also said that if his meeting with Netaji was revealed and the Indian leader did not surface he would be left clutching at straws. Goswami also told the Khosla Commission, rather dramatically, 'if Dr Radhakrishnan denies that he told me all this I will commit suicide.' Goswami also said (but did not reveal how he knew) that Vijayalakshmi Pandit had also seen Netaji in Moscow when she was posted there as India's ambassador. On her return to New Delhi, at a meeting in the Constitution Club, Pandit announced that she had some important information which if revealed would electrify the whole country. At this stage her brother Prime Minister Nehru, who was sitting next to her, pulled her sari and made her sit down, thereby silencing her.

If Stalin was still circumspect about the need to build relations with independent India, his death removed any hindrances to this possibility. Under his successor Nikita Khrushchev, the Soviet Union and India came closer and the first bilateral trade agreement was signed in 1953. The countries needed each other. India wanted machinery and cooperation for economic and industrial development that the West was chary of providing. The Soviet Union needed an ally in this part of the world where the United States was propping up Pakistan and Sino–Soviet relations were rather tense. Khrushchev did not have ideological prejudices against India and Stalinist reservations began to melt away. The new bosses at the Kremlin began to view India as a great civilization with great potential as one of the largest countries of Asia. Nehru arrived in Moscow in June 1955 on a state visit which was followed in November and December that year with return visits by Nikolai Bulganin, Soviet Premier and Khrushchev who was the general secretary of the Soviet Communist Party. The Soviet Union also began to endorse India's policy of Panchsheel—five principles of peaceful co-existence and non-alignment. This implies that even if Netaji still stood a remote chance of receiving justice at the time of Stalin's passing, in the new era of Indo–Soviet bonhomie he was at best forgotten.

The important question to ask would be: in the course of the Indo–Soviet entente, why did Nehru fail to lobby for the release of Netaji? This is a sixty-four-dollar question that will come up later in this book. Suffice to say, a request from Nehru would not have gone unheeded by the Soviet bosses, even Stalin. When Radhakrishnan first met Stalin he had raised the issue of the Moscow Radio correspondent stationed in New Delhi providing imperfect reports about goings on in India. Stalin had immediately told his aide who was present to 'call him back.' This is a good example of Stalin taking quick cognizance of an Indian request. So, why not in the case of Netaji?

Stalin probably never received any request from the India's post-Independence leaders to set Netaji free, but what did Stalin have against him that impelled him to keep the Indian leader in jail? There are no easy answers what with documents from the archives of the erstwhile Soviet Union still not fully declassified. The answer may lie in the nature of the Stalinist state. Marx had propounded his philosophy of 'from each according to his abilities to each according to his needs.' But in practice, the Soviet Union was a gargantuan state, mirroring imperialistic Czarist Russia.

The state was exploitative and freely used conscripted labour to build the resources of the country. In fact the Soviet gulags, the massive system of forced labour camps found in Siberia, was filled with prisoners only to exploit their labour. Siberia with its hostile terrain and weather suddenly became very important to the Soviet state when huge deposits of gold and platinum were discovered there in the early 1920s. Stalin wanted to exploit these minerals to generate resources to fund his five-year plans. But Siberia was remote, 6,000 km from Moscow and had no connectivity. Roads were required and mining stations had to be set up. Political dissidents from states absorbed into the the Soviet Union (like Ukraine) who resisted Communist rule, common criminals and others were forcibly conscripted. At its peak between 1940 and 1950, about 80,000 to 200,000 labourers worked in the gulags. The conditions of work were harsh and many died due to exhaustion and sicknesses. Others were shot dead for not working hard enough. An estimated half a million perished in the gulags during this period. Prisoners who died while working were buried under the roads that were then being built. For this reason, the Kolyma Highway that leads out of Yakutsk towards the west en route to Moscow, gained notoriety as Siberia's 'Road of Bones'.

Living conditions at gulags have been graphically described in Alexander Solzhenitsyn's *Gulag Archipelago*. The author had himself been locked up there for eleven years. Incidentally Yakutsk (where Netaji was interned as per Satya Narayan Sinha's testimony) is the coldest place in the world with temperatures plunging to 50 degrees below freezing temperatures in winters. So cold it is that even taking off spectacles can peel off the skin.

The Soviet Union under Stalin was a totalitarian state, exploitative and extremely cruel. Stalin sent many of his close aides to their deaths suspecting their loyalty. The most well-known is Leon Trotsky, Marxist thinker, Soviet politician and the founder and first leader of the Red Army. Thousands were eliminated in purges in the name of their being enemies of the state. This also included Red Army generals. As mentioned earlier in this chapter, even Indian Communists like Abani Mukherjee and Virendra Nath Chattopadhaya, the younger brother of Sarojini Naidu, who had been attracted by the movement also lost their lives in Stalin's jails. Stalin also used blatant force to collectivise agriculture and rapidly industrialize the country and those who resisted were bulldozed. Thus there was little value for life and sensitivity in Stalin's Russia. In these circumstances Netaji Subhas Chandra Bose may have just been reduced to a statistic in the Soviet penal system. To use an analogy from Indian prison conditions, Netaji's position was like that of an extremely poor man, languishing in jail without a trial for years together without any succour. It was as if in an insensitive jail system his case file had been lost and he had no lawyer or well-wisher outside to ring the bell of justice.

So did Netaji survive Stalin's gulag? Or does he lie buried under the 'Road of Bones'? We have no way of knowing although it is a possibility that he did survive. But before we go on to that story—based on evidence that is still very thin and does not have many takers—it is instructive to figure out another aspect. Why did others who could have saved Netaji not move to bail him out of the situation that he was in? This would include his own family and others in India including those from his native Bengal. This is the story that we will read in the next chapter.

4
Why Nobody Lobbied for Netaji's Freedom

The Bose's were a huge clan. Subhas Chandra Bose had thirteen siblings, seven brothers and six sisters, not unusual in the early years of the twentieth-century. Amongst them, Subhas was politically closest to his second eldest brother, Sarat Chandra Bose. A barrister-at-law, Sarat was eight years older to Subhas and after practicing law for many years, joined politics and involved himself in the Independence movement. In 1936 he became the president of the Bengal Provincial Congress Committee and served as an All India Congress Committee (AICC) member from 1936 to 1947. He was a leader of the Congress delegation to the Central Legislative Assembly, the chamber of elected and appointed Indian and British representatives created by the Government of India Act, 1919. In 1946 this was to give way to the Constituent Assemblies of India and Pakistan. An interim Indian government was formed with the Viceroy's Executive Council transformed into a council of ministers. It was headed by Nehru as Vice-President of the Council and he was vested with the powers of a prime minister. In 1946, a few months after Subhas had gone missing, Sarat was appointed a member of the interim government and was put in charge of Works, Mines and Power. In this way Sarat became a man of influence although quite a bit of this lustre came by way of association with his illustrious younger brother.

Sarat Chandra Bose was under detention when news about the air crash first broke out in August 1945. He found it hard to believe the story, especially as it was announced on 23 August 1945, five days after the supposed crash. An air crash makes for instantaneous news. Sarat would have found it strange that the announcement was delayed. Once out of detention he sought out Habibur Rahman to get an assessment from the ground. Netaji's comrade-in-arms stuck to the script that he had been tutored to repeat. He told Sarat Bose, 'The tragic news of Netaji's death is unfortunately true.' Rahman was a man of sterling character and there was no reason to doubt his intentions. Sarat came to the only logical conclusion, that Rahman was circulating this story on the instructions of his leader, who wanted to keep his whereabouts secret. Decades later, in the course of a parliamentary speech, Sarat's son, Subrata Bose reminisced: 'My father met Habibur Rahman for two and a half hours. After coming out of the meeting he said, "Habibur is not speaking the truth".' Habibur Rahman had also briefed Mahatma Gandhi on Netaji's death. When the Mahatma was quizzed by the press on what had transpired, he had given a cryptic reply, 'Habibur told me what his leader had ordered him to say.' Significantly when news first broke about the air crash, Mahatma Gandhi sent a telling telegram to the eldest among the Bose brothers, Satish Chandra, 'don't perform *shradh* (post-death ceremonies).' Even the Mahatma had his doubts about Netaji's death.

The tenuous nature of the air crash theory was confirmed to Sarat Bose from another completely unrelated source. On a trip to Europe in 1948 Sarat met a journalist who had been in Japan at the time the country surrendered at the end of World War II. Lily Abegg, who was a correspondent of the Zurich-based Swiss weekly, *Die Weltwoche* told Sarat that she had contacted many important British and American sources while researching on the air crash and none of them believed of the accident that was supposed to have killed Netaji.

After this Sarat Bose became even more suspicious about the air crash theory. But he had been a little miffed with his younger brother when stories came to him that Subhas had married his secretary in Austria in 1938, much before he escaped from home in 1941 and that he had a daughter. Sarat had known nothing about this and he was upset that Subhas had kept him in the dark. Congress circles had been rife with rumours about Netaji's live-in relationship which caused the elder Bose further angst. In the context of the conservative social mores of those times, this was nothing short of a scandal, which found the Bose family on the defensive. Many in the family even wondered whether the daughter was actually Netaji's. The matter was resolved when the daughter came to Calcutta many years later. Suresh Bose saw the girl and had tears in his eyes. He said, 'Look at her face. She has to be a Bose family girl', and started weeping.

Sarat Bose was unaware that Netaji's wife Emilie Schenkl had written to him on 12 March 1946 regarding her marriage to Subhas in 1937 and the birth of their daughter in November 1942. Emilie wrote that she was in possession of a copy of a letter that Netaji had written to Sarat Bose on his marriage. He had obviously feared that one day he would not be in a position to tell Sarat about his wife. Emilie's letter reached Sarat only two years later: it had been intercepted by British intelligence, which instead of forwarding it to Sarat, had begun circulating rumours about Subhas and his companion in Congress party circles. Sarat wrote back to Emilie on 10 April 1948 addressing her as Mrs Schenkl. He said, 'It is difficult these days to trust many people here. Most of the eminent Congress leaders were political enemies of my brother and tried their best to run him down. The attitude does not seem to have changed even after all that happened after 1941.' He also promised to visit Vienna, where she lived and meet her. The copy of the letter was published in the 10 February 2014 issue of the Indian newsmagazine *Outlook*. In the event, Sarat Bose called on Emilie in Vienna with his family and requested her to move to Calcutta to stay with them. But Emilie had her own mother to look after and politely declined the offer.

Sarat, on his part, was disenchanted with the Congress party which he felt had lost its moorings and was besieged by corruption and nepotism. He resigned from the AICC over his disagreement on the partition of Bengal. He and Muslim League leader Huseyn Shaheed Suhrawardy had wanted a united, independent Bengal. It was felt that this would keep the economy of Bengal intact. The Partition brought in its wake untold miseries and a series of communal conflagrations in Bengal. As millions of refugees poured into West Bengal from East Pakistan the political discourse changed and began to devolve around how to rehabilitate the displaced persons in West Bengal.

In the midst of conflicting reports about the survival of Netaji it was becoming increasingly difficult for Sarat Bose to get to the truth of his brother's disappearance. Out of the Congress and echelons of power he had no way of knowing that the new Nehru government had begun to assiduously court Stalin. In those days although stories were floating that Netaji may have escaped to the Soviet Union nobody would have imagined that he was held under inhuman conditions. In fact the outside world knew little about the gulags, the existence of which came to light only after the death of Stalin. So there was no question of Sarat Bose having tried to get Subhas Bose out of imprisonment in the Soviet Union. Sarat did not live too long. He passed away on 20 February 1950, three weeks after India became a Republic.

In the early 1950s as the country settled down after Partition and took baby steps as a Republic, questions about the whereabouts of Netaji began to be raised again. If his presence in Russia had only been speculated upon in the period 1946 to 1948, now this view became a little more prominent. A Member of Parliament from the Forward Bloc H.V. Kamath led the voices calling for clarity on the whereabouts of Subhas Bose. The government was not open to investigating the matter. In reply to a query by Kamath, the Deputy Minister for External Affairs, Balakrishna Vishwanath Keskar, in a written reply in the Lok Sabha on 19 April 1951 said, 'government have not received any special communication or news or any kind of evidence which might lead to the possibility of Subhas Chandra Bose being alive.' Keskar recalled the statement made by Nehru in 1946 that, 'after due enquiry for collection of whatever evidence that was possible there was little doubt that Subhas Bose had died on 18 August 1945.' Keskar's submission in Parliament added that the stated conclusion was confirmed by reports from the Japanese government which included a medical report on the leader's death. But Kamath was insistent and wanted an inquiry into the matter. Two months later, on 5 March 1952, Nehru himself answered a question from Kamath. He said, 'I have no doubt in my mind and I did not have then and I have no doubt today of the fact of Subhas Chandra Bose's death. There can be no enquiry at all.' It does seem that Nehru was eager for a final resolution over the question of Netaji's disappearance as can be gleaned from a note which was quoted by Subrata Bose when he spoke on the subject in Parliament in 2006. In the official note dated 26 September 1951 Nehru had written, 'It is for us to consider whether we should issue a public statement or not about this (Netaji's death). On the balance I am inclined to think that it would be desirable to issue some statement or make it in Parliament. This may lead to some controversy even with Shri Subhas Chandra Bose's family. I think that the best course would be for us to draft some such statement and to send it to Shri Subhas Chandra Bose's family. After hearing from them, we could take a final decision about the publication.'

No statement was ever made. The reason for this appears to be caution, as advised by the then foreign secretary, K.P.S. Menon. He wrote on 27 September 1951, 'I told the PM that it would be inadvisable to make a statement now. I think that there is significant reference in Habibur Rahman's statement to Netaji Bose's intention to get off the plane at Dairen and to the intention of the Japanese authority to let him cross over to Russian held territory.' The foreign secretary, it seems, was also hinting that there were multiple versions—he pointed out that while Habibur Rahman had said that the departed leader was cremated on 20 August 1945, the municipal certificate put the date of cremation at 22 August 1945. The foreign secretary wondered of the need for a fictitious date for the cremation. With conflicting dates extant, Menon was probably trying to say that no purpose would be served by putting out a version whose credibility could be called to question easily.

Realizing that the Nehru government was adamant in stalling any investigation on the disappearance of Netaji, civil society representatives thought that an unofficial committee could always be set up to go into the matter. Suresh Chandra Bose proposed the name of international jurist Radhabinod Pal as head of the committee. Pal had made a name for himself as a member of the international tribunal that tried Japanese war criminals—and as had been stated in an earlier chapter—had found all of them 'not guilty'. More importantly Pal, a former Calcutta High Court judge had spent many months in Tokyo for the tribunal and had used that opportunity to speak to important officers of the Allied forces. His understanding: nobody believed that Netaji had died in the purported air crash. In fact an American member of the tribunal had shown him a copy of the report of the American intelligence agency party which had visited Taihoku in September 1945. According to this report there was no air crash in Taihoku and that Subhas Chandra Bose had safely made his way to Dairen on 18 August 1945.

At this point in 1956 Nehru (who had been against the inquiry all along) got into the act and proposed the name of Shah Nawaz Khan to head the committee. His reasoning: Khan was a former member of the INA top-brass who had faced trial at Red Fort which implied that his credibility would be high. But there was criticism against the co-option of Khan who was a parliamentary secretary in the Nehru government and could not be seen as independent. Since the Committee was an informal one, Nehru proposed that the West Bengal government should also nominate a representative of the Bengalis, Bengal being the state where Netaji's influence was the maximum. Thus S.N. Maitra, an Indian Civil Service officer, was appointed to the Committee. Nehru also induced Suresh Chandra Bose to join as a representative of Netaji's family. Shortly after the Committee was conceived it became an official body.

Suresh Chandra Bose like his elder brother Sarat Chandra Bose and other family members was in two minds about whether Netaji had survived the air crash. But once he began investigating he realized that there was much more to the matter. The air crash had never taken place. So, where was the question of his younger brother having died? In the course of the Committee hearings, Suresh came to the conclusion that Netaji had indeed used Japanese contacts to push into Russian territory and surrendered there as per plan. Some contradictory statements by supposed eyewitnesses who deposed before the Committee caught his attention. Three of the Japanese witnesses said that they were navigators of the plane. But when asked where the crew sat in the plane, they were blank. One of the witnesses even said, 'we got down from the plane in Taipei and after that the plane took off with Netaji.'

The other two members had not realized that Suresh would take an independent line and tried to bring him around to the majority view—that an air crash had taken place and Netaji had perished in the accident. But Suresh was fired by the memory of his brother: he had been close to Subhas who was just about five years younger than him. In large families with scores of members, siblings often would be distant from each other. But it so happened that Subhas and Suresh stayed together in the Elgin Road house of the Boses in Calcutta, even as many other brothers had shifted out elsewhere—and this included Sarat Bose who stayed in a separate house. Starting his working life as a magistrate in Orissa (Odisha), Suresh had quit his job after being forced by a senior to write a judgment against a nationalist. Thereafter he went to Germany and studied glass technology. Back home he dabbled in the refrigeration business and transportation of perishables like fish from East Bengal and from Chilika Lake in Orissa to West Bengal, but with poor success. Suresh may have been a poor businessman but certainly a man to call a spade a spade. He had married his daughter to a boy working for INA's secret service—in fact his son-in-law was sentenced to death for aiding Subhas' organization but let off at the last moment after Mahatma Gandhi pleaded for clemency.

When efforts were being made to cajole Suresh Bose into the broad points of a general agreement that Netaji died in the air crash, he revolted and complained to Nehru. The prime minister, instead of taking cognizance of Suresh's letter of 13 August 1956, replied, 'it is difficult to understand what you have written'. Nehru added that Shah Nawaz Khan and S.N. Maitra had come to meet him on 3 August and said that Suresh Bose had left Delhi 'without writing the report.'

Suresh Bose had informed Nehru that he wanted to write a dissenting view and for that he needed access to the witness statements and other documents that the Committee had collected. Nehru refused this access saying that the Committee had already submitted the report and now they were part of the records of the external affairs ministry. Thus the records could not be given to Suresh; he would have to come to Delhi and could 'see the documents', nothing more. In fact the *Dissentient Report* was supposed to be part of the main report though this was never allowed and was published separately. As a result of his investigative labours a lot of people who had doubts about Netaji's demise realized that the air crash story was bogus. More importantly the members of the Bose family also began veering around to this point of view.

These were the times when Nehru's popularity was enormous: he was going from strength to strength. With the demise of Sardar Vallabhbhai Patel in 1950, who had a tempering influence on Nehru's assuming unbridled power, it was as if the prime minister's words were virtually law. In these circumstances for the Bose family to be heard was almost impossible. It was Sarat's son, Amiya Nath, a lawyer who kept up the demand for unravelling the Netaji mystery, even suggesting the matter be handed over to the Chief Justice of India. As usual Nehru stalled the matter. A few weeks before his death in a letter to Amiya dated 22 April 1964 Nehru said, 'I agree with you that something should be done to finalise the question of Netaji's death. But it is not clear to me how far it will be proper for me to ask the Chief Justice of India to look into this matter.' Suresh Chandra Bose had also kept pursuing the matter and had a rather telling communication from Nehru. He had asked Nehru to show him conclusive proof of the death of Netaji. In a letter dated 13 May 1962, Nehru had replied, 'You asked me to send you proof of the death of Netaji Subhas Chandra Bose. I cannot send you any precise proof.'

It was not just Nehru's overwhelming influence that queered the pitch for the demand into an investigation into Netaji's disappearance. Partition left in its wake a badly divided Congress and excised much of Bengal—the province where Subhas Bose' influence was felt the most. The Congress party that represented the voice of the people was falling into the control of non-political persons who were little other than acolytes of Nehru. Bidhan Chandra Roy was West Bengal's chief minister for fourteen years. Roy was reputed to be an excellent doctor and had two prestigious British medical fellowships under his belt—he was both Member of the Royal College of Physicians as well as Fellow of the Royal College of Surgeons. It was said that his nose for diagnosis was so strong that he would just have to glance at a patient to figure out the ailment. He was also a freedom fighter but then he had little political acumen and as chief minister he was merely a representative of the Delhi durbar. He could not articulate the aspirations of the growing stream of displaced persons from East Bengal and rehabilitate them, much less satisfactorily take up the issue of the disappearance of Netaji.

After Independence, the Communist Party of India was on the rise and with their traditional link with the Soviet Union they could have brought the matter of Netaji centre stage. But they had little interest in Netaji. In fact Subhas Chandra Bose was their favourite whipping boy during World War II. Because of his alliance with the Germans, the Communists used to berate Netaji for being a fascist. They also used to denigrate him for his association with the Japanese and lampoon him as 'Tojo's dog' (Japanese Prime Minister Hideki Tojo) and as a traitor and a quisling. The Communists in India started revising their opinion about Subhas Bose only in the late 1970s. In the fifties, when they could have significantly added weight to the search for Netaji, they continued to hold the same opinion about the Indian leader. They did not lean on the Soviets to open the doors for a search.

In the early 1950s if there was any parliamentarian who could take on Nehru squarely it was Syama Prasad Mookerjee. Fed up with Nehru's policies he wanted to set up a national development alternative to the Congress since it was felt that the party had not dealt with the problem of Partition properly. In 1951, Syama Prasad set up the Indian People's Party, soon to become the Bharatiya Jana Sangh. Syama Prasad, also from Calcutta could have effectively taken up the issue of Netaji even though they were from different ideological backgrounds. But Syama Prasad died mysteriously in June 1953 in Srinagar while under detention. Thus another quarter from where pressure to unravel the mystery could have been mounted was extinguished.

What about the INA men? Why did they not exert pressure on the government of the day to unravel the mystery of disappearance of their former boss? The Nehru government did the very best to obliterate the memory of the INA and marginalize their rank and file. In such circumstances there was no question of their being able to raise their voices. When India became independent there was talk of inducting the INA men who had been put up on trial into the Indian Army. They had all been part of the British Indian Army but had been cashiered after the War. Nehru had wanted free India to be a successor state to British India. So there was no question of re-inducting these men into the Indian Army. They would have brought their independent views into the army which carried on with all the trappings of the colonial forces. Nehru had consulted his bureaucrats and army officers on this matter. The former were all from the colonial Indian Civil Service. As to the latter they were officers like the Sandhurst-trained General Satyawant Mallannah Shrinagesh, the third chief of the Indian Army in independent India. They were all against incorporating the INA men. Some of the

INA men were inducted into politics like Shah Nawaz Khan but they quickly learnt to be on the right side of the new establishment. General Jayanto Nath Chaudhuri who became Chief of Army Staff in 1962 succinctly summarised the state of affairs in a lecture on Nehru and the Indian armed forces that he delivered in 1973 many years after superannuation. He said, 'The INA men were not reinstated and though some benefits were paid to them and a very few political appointments having no connection with the armed forces were made available to some of them, their treatment was in fact surprisingly cool after all the adulation that they received a year earlier.'

J.K. Bhonsle, INA's chief of staff and one of Netaji's key aides is a good example of how the former members of the INA fell in line. After Independence, Bhonsle became deputy minister in the Nehru government and went by the official line that Netaji had died in the air crash. In any case he chose to keep his own counsel. This was the same Bhonsle who had been interrogated by the Combined Services Detailed Interrogation Centre (India) at the Red Fort in March 1946 at the behest of the Intelligence Bureau. The Bureau thought that he knew more than what he had earlier revealed: that Netaji had left for Tokyo on 17 August. On interrogation he had revealed that he was part of a closed door meeting with 'Netaji, Habibur Rahman and Japanese officials that discussed how to get Bose to his destination.' He revealed that it was Subhas Bose's intention to try to find his way into Russia and that Bose was certain that once the Russians agreed to allow him in, they would give all the necessary protection. Bhonsle also said that in the event of an Anglo-American split with Russia, which Bose definitely foresaw, he could be of some service to the Russians which in turn would further the case of his country. A.C.N. Nambiar, Netaji's deputy in Germany also joined the post-Independence establishment. After Independence he served as Counsellor to the Indian Legation in Switzerland, then India's ambassador to Scandinavia and ultimately to the Federal Republic of Germany. Anand Mohan Sahay, another minister of the Azad

Hind government, after serving as Consul-General of India in some South-east Asian countries was appointed as India's ambassador to Thailand. Shah Nawaz Khan progressed rapidly after heading the Netaji enquiry committee and served as a cabinet minister in Congress governments well after the death of Nehru. Settled well in life, Netaji, who once inspired them for a higher cause remained a mere memory.

5

The Rise of Subhas

Resigning from the Indian Civil Service (ICS) in May 1921, Subhas Chandra Bose set sail for India. Bose, then twenty-four, had cleared the ICS examinations conducted the previous year and had stood fourth. But with news trickling in about the non-cooperation movement in India initiated by the Congress, the emerging leader realized where his calling lay. The programme adopted in December 1920 had made a call for renunciation of titles and resignation from government jobs and was marked by the picketing of British goods and use of locally manufactured cloth. Bose had instinctively understood that as a civil servant he could not serve two masters—the British government, and the people— at the same time.

A day after disembarking at Bombay (Mumbai), Bose went to see Mahatma Gandhi who was then staying at Mani Bhavan in the city. It was the afternoon of 16 July 1921. Bose was ushered into the presence of the Mahatma who welcomed him with a hearty smile and straightaway put his visitor at ease. The impatient Subhas—who was raring to go—started firing off question after question in rapid succession. The Mahatma answered with his habitual patience. As Bose has related in his book *The Indian Struggle* he had, in essence, three sets of questions. The first: how would the different activities of the Congress (under the non-cooperation movement) culminate in the last stage of campaign, namely the non-payment of taxes? Secondly, how would the non-payment of taxes or civil disobedience force out the British government and leave Indians free to govern themselves? Thirdly, what was the basis of Gandhi's promise that India could attain *swaraj* (self-rule) within a year if the non-cooperation programme was fully implemented?

Bose was disappointed with Gandhi's answers, except the first one, and later related in his memoirs, 'I had desired to obtain a clear understanding of the details—the successive stages—of his plan.' He was clearly dissatisfied and noted, 'My reason told me clearly, again and again, that there was a deplorable lack of clarity in the plan which the Mahatma had formulated and that he himself did not have a clear idea of the successive stages of campaign which would bring India to her cherished goal of freedom.' In the footnotes he added, almost as an afterthought, that the Mahatma was probably relying on a change of heart amongst the British to leave India.

Bose's disappointment must have shown on his face because Gandhi asked him to report to Deshbandhu Chittaranjan Das in Calcutta. Bose dutifully met Das immediately after reaching Calcutta. A barrister with a roaring practice, Das had given it up the previous year to serve the nation. Das was not in town and Bose called on him again a few days later. He notes in his memoirs how his 'mind was made up' after the meeting. Bose writes, 'I felt that I had found a leader and I meant to follow him.' Bose began to work with Das, effectively kick-starting his own political career.

It was not long before he had his first taste of jail. The Prince of Wales was slated to visit India on the eve of Christmas 1921 and a month ahead of the event Das and Bose successfully organized a dress rehearsal of a boycott that they were planning against the British royal. The boycott was very successful and sparked off public enthusiasm. But the English-owned English-language papers *The Statesman* and *Englishman* taunted the government for allowing 'the Congress volunteers to take possession of the city.' Little wonder then that for their impertinence the duo were arrested that December and sentenced to six months imprisonment.

The non-cooperation movement that started in 1920 was brought to an abrupt end in 1922 after the Chauri Chaura incident. On 5 February 1922 a group of protesters taking part in the Civil Disobedience Movement, provoked by police firing on them, attacked and burnt a police station at Chauri Chaura in Gorakhpur district of United Provinces, killing twenty-three policeman and three civilians. Gandhi immediately called off the peaceful non-cooperation movement although large numbers of Congressmen were against such a move. Bose, who was disenchanted with Gandhi from day one, says in his book that 'to sound the order of retreat just when public enthusiasm was reaching the boiling point was nothing short of a national calamity.' He said that popular Congress leaders like Chittaranjan Das, Motilal Nehru and Lala Lajpat Rai shared this public resentment but they were all in jail. Bose adds that Rai in anguish wrote a seventy-page letter to Gandhi where among other things he challenged the idea of Ahimsa as propagated by the Mahatma and declared it to be an act of cowardice and unmanliness.

Now active sections of Congressmen led by Chittaranjan Das proposed that the party should continue non-cooperation by entering the legislative assemblies and blocking government moves. But the no-changer group supported by Gandhi won the day at the annual session of the Congress held at Gaya in 1922. Das was president of the Congress at this time and quit in protest. Subsequently he started the Swaraj Party (within the Congress fold) along with other members in favour of non-cooperation.

Around this time elections for the newly formed Calcutta Corporation that incorporated the adjacent municipalities of Cossipore, Manicktola, Chitpore and Garden Reach were held and in April 1924 Chittaranjan Das became the first elected Mayor of Calcutta. Bose was appointed as the chief executive officer of the Corporation and would assist Das in running the municipal administration. The appointment raised many eyebrows because Bose was just about twenty-seven. But Das was sure of his choice. He knew that his protégé was a young man with calibre, dedication and purpose.

In those days the levers of influence in Bengal society were held by the three Hindu upper castes: the Brahmins, Baidyas and the Kayasthas. The Muslims, numerically the largest group, had been disempowered for many decades and had begun to be conscious of their status. There was an undercurrent of feeling among them. They too wanted their just place under the sun. This feeling of deprivation would often boil over and aggravate tensions between Hindus and Muslims. Chittaranjan Das understood this and figured out that a sound future for the province could only be ensured by according the Muslims their rightful place. In a radical move he conceived of an accord with the Muslims that allowed for greater representation for them in the legislative assembly and local bodies. It was decided that, henceforth, 50 per cent of all appointments to government jobs would go to Muslims. Moreover till the Muslims attained this level of representation, 80 per cent of the jobs would be filled by the community. The Bengal Pact of 1923, as this accord was named, was decried by moderate Hindu leaders like Surendra Nath Banerjee who held sway over public opinion. They felt that the Hindu upper caste influence would reduce. But Das stuck to his guns and with Bose as his able assistant went around recruiting Muslims to fill 80 per cent of the jobs for which hiring was taking place in the Corporation. At that time Muslims made up for hardly 18 per cent of the positions in the Corporation. The Muslims hailed Das even as the pact was cleared by the Bengal Pradesh Congress Committee (BPCC) at its meeting on 18 December 1923. Das' popularity was at its zenith and he became the uncrowned king of Bengal.

Along with the Muslims, Das also stayed in touch with the revolutionaries of Bengal who had turned out to be a thorn in the side of the British. Bose too maintained contact with them and was quite upfront about it.

Charles Tegart, the Commissioner of Calcutta Police was a notorious man, known for his harsh ways. In January 1924, a revolutionary named Gopinath Saha sought to kill him, but instead shot down Ernest Day, an English commercial manager. Saha was arrested and convicted to death by hanging. But on Bose's prompting the BPCC passed a qualified resolution in support of Saha. A similar proposal was passed by the Corporation. The resolution appreciated Saha's courage and spirit of sacrifice although it condemned the act of killing. Needless to add this brought Bose into focus and the British decided that he was too dangerous a man to be allowed to continue with his political activities.

In the early hours of the morning of 25 October 1924 Bose was roused from his sleep by policemen carrying a warrant of arrest. It had been issued under Regulation III of 1818 that allowed the police to arrest anyone and detain them indefinitely. Empowered by another warrant the police searched the Bose residence for any arms stowed away for revolutionary activity. Nothing was found. That there could be arms and ammunition in Bose's residence was a ruse. The government was unnerved by the activities of the members of the Swaraj Party which was quite radical in its approach and was more in the face in its approach than the Congress party. According to Bose's memoirs the Corporation was running smoothly and the citizens were happy. It is possible that this could have irked the ruling establishment. That morning, many other Congressmen were also arrested.

To avoid adverse public reaction, Bose was driven to the police headquarters in his car by the English deputy commissioner of police and from there to Calcutta's Alipore Central Jail. Bose continued his work as chief executive officer of the Corporation from within the jail. His secretary would visit him now and then with the necessary files. This upset the British authorities so much that they transferred him to Berhampore Jail away from Calcutta. This was not to be his final destination. Two months later, in December 1924, Bose was transferred back to Alipore Central Jail and from there transported to the infamous Mandalay Prison in Upper Burma (Myanmar). This was a prison reserved for especially troublesome Indian political prisoners. Bal Gangadhar 'Lokmanya' Tilak, Lala Lajpat Rai and Sardar Ajit Singh had served time here. There were other Indian political prisoners incarcarated there along with Bose.

It was only two and a half years later, on 16 May 1927 that Bose was released from captivity. He had stood for elections to the Bengal Legislative Council from jail hoping that a victory would force his captors to release him. He went on to win a thumping majority but continued to be in detention. In the interim, he had also served time in Insein Jail, where he was transferred after some trouble with the jail authorities in Mandalay. His health had deteriorated in captivity, his lungs were badly affected by a bronchial attack leading to tuberculosis. Although it seemed sensible to release him, the British authorities were too scared to set him free. They proposed that Bose set sail to Switzerland from Rangoon to rest and recuperate at a sanatorium, without a stopover in Calcutta. He refused to go along with this proposal. In the end the British thought it would make sense to send him off to Almora in the Indian Himalayas and he was brought to Calcutta en-route. Here, the British had a change of heart and Bose was released. He was barely thirty.

The political scene in Bengal had changed a lot. Chittaranjan Das had passed away suddenly in 1925 leaving a void among the Bengal nationalists. This most towering leader of Bengal, who had held disparate forces together, was there no more to minister to his flock. The conservative elements in the Congress party seized their chance to repudiate the Bengal Pact that Das had so assiduously nurtured. This drew howls of protest from Muslims who realized that they would have to look out for their hopes for the future in other political formations. The rejection of the Pact at the annual conference of the BPCC in 1926 at Krishnanagar set the tone for the division of Bengal nineteen years later.

The man who was now trying hard to capture the leadership of the Congress in Bengal was Jatindra Mohan Sengupta who was cast in the Gandhian mould and was an ardent follower of the Mahatma. A barrister, Sengupta had been to jail many times and was just forty-two in 1927, the year Bose returned home from prison in Burma. Thus Sengupta too was fairly young and the next six years saw considerable friction between the two leaders from Bengal, with each trying to outmanoeuvre the other. The ensuing tension came to a close only with Sengupta's premature death in a Ranchi prison in 1933.

In 1928, possibly to emphasize his political philosophy and demonstrate how different it was from that of Sengupta and his mentor Gandhi, Bose appeared in military attire as the general-officer-commanding of the Bengal Volunteers at the Congress session held in Calcutta. This captured the attention of the youth and Bose was back in the political limelight. He would soon become a recognised figure across the country.

In this period the factional fights in the Bengal Congress had intensified. Sengupta complained to the Congress leadership that Bose had manipulated the district Congress committees in such a way as to influence the choice of the All-India Congress Committee (AICC) representatives from Bengal. Party leader Bhogaraju Pattabhi Sitaramayya was deputed to inquire into the matter which was followed up by a visit from Congress president Motilal Nehru who ordered fresh elections to the AICC from Bengal. The clashes within the Bengal Congress failed to die down and in fact the differences-in-opinion within the Bengal Congress seem to have gone pretty deep. Sengupta, who was the Mayor of Calcutta resigned from his position after being arrested for reading out 'seditious literature' in public. When fresh elections were being held he indicated that he was in favour of the joint candidate for the Muslim and European councillors, Prince Golam Mohammad Shah. This was in spite of the fact that his fellow party member Bose was also a candidate. In the end Subhas was elected to the Mayor's post on 22 August 1930. He had participated in this election from within the precincts of Calcutta's Alipore Central Jail after being arrested in January that year. He was released from prison only a month after winning the election—on 23 September 1930—and sworn in as Mayor the next day.

In recognition of his countrywide stature, Bose was nominated to the committee chaired by Motilal Nehru in 1929 to draft a report on the principles for a new Constitution of India. This exercise was being undertaken by the Congress to undercut the Simon Commission that had been set up by the British government to suggest constitutional reforms for India. The Simon Commission was boycotted because it had no Indian members. The Motilal Nehru Committee made far-reaching recommendations—it pitched for universal franchise and elections through a joint electorate of all communities. It recommended reservation of seats for minorities for ten years (except in Bengal and Punjab where Muslims were in a majority), autonomy for provinces and a bicameral system of a Senate and House of Representatives.

The battle for India's freedom took a new turn in December 1929 at the annual session of the Congress party, in Lahore under the presidency of Jawaharlal Nehru which passed a resolution for *Poorna Swaraj* or complete independence. Nehru and Bose represented the more radical sections of the Congress party in those days—Nehru was forty-one years old and Netaji was thirty-three. The formal demand for *Poorna Swaraj* came after a year of internal struggle within the Congress.

In December 1928, at the Congress session in Calcutta, Mahatma Gandhi had proposed a resolution calling for the British to grant dominion status to India within two years. It was decided that if the British failed the deadline, the Congress would call upon all the Indians to fight for complete independence. But Bose and Nehru objected to the resolution, they pressed Mahatma Gandhi for immediate action. Gandhi then proposed a resolution reducing the time given from two years to one. Nehru voted for the new resolution and fell in line but Bose abstained. Ultimately the AICC passed the resolution 118 to 95. Soon thereafter Bose moved an amendment at an open session that sought a complete break with the British. Gandhi admonished Bose and their differences became public. Gandhi's word carried more weight: the amendment was defeated.

The *Poorna Swaraj* resolution was formally promulgated with a 'Declaration of Independence' by Mahatma Gandhi on 26 January 1930, the day declared as Independence Day by the Congress. This time round Gandhi gave the British two months to leave India. When the foreign rulers ignored this missive as had been expected, Gandhi wrote to the Viceroy Lord Irwin on 2 March 1930 informing him of his intent to launch a non-violent civil disobedience movement. On 12 March 1930, Gandhi along with seventy-eight followers set out from the Sabarmati Ashram in Ahmedabad on a 241-mile *padayatra*—journey on foot—to the coastal village of Dandi in south Gujarat. The history of the Dandi March or Salt Satyagraha is too well known to be recounted here. It raised national and international consciousness about the brutality and insensitivity of the British regime. Batches of passive resistors would march forward to break the law and collect sea water to produce salt even as policemen rained blows upon them.

The British Empire stood exposed like never before. Gandhi was arrested but realizing that they were on the back foot, the Mahatma was invited to join the second Round Table Conference in London, where representatives from other political parties and the Indian princely states were invited. The Conference held between September and December 1931 had no concrete outcome. The Congress had boycotted the first conference held between November 1930 and January 1931. In effect the Civil Disobedience Movement had come to naught. India was no closer to independence than it had been before the Salt Satyagraha. The Congress hierarchy was frustrated and rather demoralised. Bose had foreseen the failure of the talks and had even forewarned Gandhi about this. Bose was incarcerated in Alipore Central Jail when the Salt Satyagraha commenced in March 1930. Such was the British anger against Indian political prisoners that Bose and others like Jatindra Mohan Sengupta, Kiron Shankar

Roy were mercilessly beaten with batons for attempting *satyagraha* in jail. Bose was thrown down and rendered unconscious for more than an hour.

On his release from jail Bose travelled to Bombay to meet Gandhi. He wanted to discuss the Delhi pact of 5 March 1931 between Irwin and Gandhi which had offered a rather vague offer of 'dominion status' for India and paved the way for the Round Table Conference later that year. Bose told the Mahatma what he thought was wrong with the pact and pointed out that nothing short of full independence was acceptable and that Gandhi should have insisted on it. He told Gandhi that this was not his personal opinion but that he was speaking for many other Congress activists. The Gandhi–Irwin Pact was ratified at the annual conference of the Congress at Karachi in 1931.

One of Bose's primary contentions was that the pact had delved into unnecessary details while avoiding the main issue of *Poorna Swaraj*. He was also opposed to the fact that Indian delegates to the Conference were to be chosen by the British government and not the Indian people. Moreover there would be no finality to the points discussed at the Round Table Conference. They would have to be discussed and ratified afresh by the British Parliament.

Bose evoked much fear in the British—they averred that he was planning an armed revolution in India—and they would not allow him to remain free and out of jail for long. In January 1932, on his way to Bombay to attend a Congress Working Committee meeting as a special invitee, he was arrested by police who stopped his train at Kalyan thirty miles short of the destination. He was shifted to Jubbulpore Jail from where he was shifted to a hospital in Lucknow after he suffered a nervous disorder. The English doctor who examined Bose said that his condition was not good and that he could survive only if he were taken to Europe. The British police put him up in a ship to Europe sailing from Bombay. He reached Vienna on 8 March 1933. The treatment was effective and the change of place improved his health and he travelled to Switzerland, Czechoslovakia, Romania, Bulgaria and Poland. It is here that he penned the first part of the two-volume *The Indian Struggle*. He wrote it quite hurriedly, relying largely on his memory, since he had no access to records abroad. He also struck up a great friendship with Vithalbhai Patel, an Indian leader and elder brother of Sardar Vallabhbhai Patel, who was also undergoing medical treatment at Vienna. When Patel passed away in Vienna, he left behind his wealth to Subhas Bose so that he could use it for the Indian cause. Patel and Bose also released a joint statement condemning the withdrawal of the Civil Disobedience Movement by Gandhi in 1934.

That Bose was very critical of Gandhi becomes clearer from a reading of *Indian Struggle*. Asking the question why Gandhi had failed to deliver freedom to India, Bose said that while the Mahatma understood 'the character of his own people, he has not understood the character of his opponents.' He added, 'We have to render unto Caesar what is Caesar's', implying that force was the only language that the British would understand. Bose also noted that Gandhi had failed because the 'false unity of interests that are inherently opposed is not a source of strength but a source of weakness in political warfare.' This means that different interest groups could align together in name but in reality would work at cross purposes and the purpose of coming together would be lost.

Subhas also noted, 'The Congress Cabinet of today is a one man show. Congress Working Committee (CWC) is undoubtedly composed of some of the finest men of India. But most of them have been chosen primarily because of their "blind" loyalty to the Mahatma and there are few among them who have the capacity to think for themselves or the desire to speak out against the Mahatma when he is likely to take a wrong step.' He lamented the premature death of Chittaranjan Das, Motilal Nehru and Lala Lajpat Rai, three outstanding intellectuals who could reason with Gandhi.

Pointing out that the Swaraj Party which operated virtually independently under the banner of the Congress party was 'frankly an anti-Gandhi party and it was strong enough to force the Mahatma to voluntary retirement from politics' for six years.

At the same time Bose conceded that Gandhi was hugely popular and attributed it to his practices of asceticism, simple life, vegetarianism and adherence to truth, which gave him a halo of saintliness. Bose also noted that the Mahatma fully exploited the weak traits in the character of his countrymen which had accounted for its downfall to a large extent. This included the inordinate belief in fate and the supernatural and indifference to modern scientific development.

In late 1934, Bose briefly returned to India to see his seriously ailing father, who however passed away before the two could meet. The British authorities then put pressure on Bose to leave India and he went back to Vienna. On the way back he disembarked at Naples onwards to Rome where he met the Italian leader Benito Mussolini in January 1935. In 1936 on the invitation of Irish president Éamon de Valera, under whose leadership Ireland had thrown off the English yoke, Subhas visited Dublin. It was clear that Bose was now seeking to forge international alliances and thinking of gathering external support to free India.

In this period, the British police were suspicious of Bose and kept a watch on him, although the Austrians were not very cooperative. At the end of 1936, Bose decided to come back to India. Getting wind of his plans, the British Consul in Vienna, J.W. Taylor wrote to Subhas, 'Government of India has seen in the press statements that you propose to return to India this month and the Government of India desires to make it clear to you that should you do so, you cannot expect to remain at liberty.'

On returning to Bombay, Bose was arrested and transferred to Kurseong near Darjeeling and detained in his brother's bungalow. His health was not showing signs of improvement and so he was sent to Calcutta Medical College and Hospital and finally released from house-arrest in 1937. As he had not fully recovered, Bose spent a few months in Dalhousie and then made a brief trip to Europe.

In the interim after calling off the Civil Disobedience Movement in 1934 Gandhi had virtually withdrawn from politics and begun to concentrate on other matters like the upliftment of Harijans. Although Gandhi's move had its own logic, that political freedom would have no meaning if not accompanied by social transition, the freedom movement was seen as lagging. London, in an initiative aimed at taking the wind out of the sails of the freedom movement had passed the Government of India Act in 1935. An elaborate and lengthy Act, it sought to give Indians some say in local self-government. The balance of power remained with the British—the Viceroy and Governors—who could intervene in matters of state whenever they wanted. As mandated by the Act, provincial elections were held in the winter of 1936–37 and the results declared in February 1937. Some 30.1 million citizens including 4.25 million women were eligible to vote. Of these 15.5 million actually voted. The Congress won 707 seats out of 1,585 and also won absolute majority in Madras, United Provinces, Central Provinces, Bihar, Orissa and Bombay. In Assam and the North-West Frontier Province (NWFP), the Congress was the largest party but in Bengal, Punjab and Sindh the situation was not too rosy for them. All the three states had a substantial Muslim population. With the Muslim League around, the Congress could not make much inroad into Muslim votes. In states ruled by princes no elections were held. In other provinces, governments were set up.

Internationally war clouds were gathering and a major conflagration was in the offing. The German invasion of Poland on 1 September 1939 set off World War II that was to last for more than six years involving some thirty countries and would leave a trail of destruction across the world. On 3 September 1939, Great Britain and France declared war on Germany. Back in India, between October and November 1939 all the Congress ministries resigned. This was in protest against the decision of the Viceroy, Lord Linlithgow, who declared India as a belligerent in the War without consulting the Indian people.

When Bose returned from the brief Europe tour in 1937 he was sounded off by the Congress leadership about a term as president of the party. The prolonged incarceration and exile forced upon him by the British, that had destroyed his health, seems to have generated sympathy among his colleagues.

6

Gandhi Coterie and Subhas Bose

Haripura is a village near Kadod town in the Surat district of Gujarat. It is on the banks of the river Tapi and close to Bardoli, which saw an agrarian Satyagraha in 1922. There is nothing exceptional about Haripura and it would not have found a place in the footnotes of history had it not been for an event of historical importance that was hosted there more than seventy years ago. In 1938, for four days between 19 and 22 February, Haripura played host to the 51st session of the Congress which elected Subhas Chandra Bose, then forty-one, party president.

According to contemporary reports, some 200,000 Congress delegates attended the annual session of the party, with Bose arriving in a chariot drawn by fifty-one bulls on the opening day. Each bull represented a year of the existence of the Congress party. 'Mammoth crowds, estimated at more than half a million people, witnessed the procession and paid homage to the President-Elect Subhas Chandra Bose,' wrote Ben Bradley, who was witness to this spectacular gathering, in the *Labour Monthly* in April 1938. By the time of this meet Bose had built a formidable reputation for himself. He had been to jail seven times in the past seventeen years, ranging from a few months to two and a half years. He had even braved the rigours of the notorious Mandalay prison in Burma where conditions were said to be abysmal.

He was released prematurely from this jail because he had contracted tuberculosis, a dangerous disease in those days. All this had added to the stature of the upcoming leader who was seen as uncompromising in his attitude to the British.

The Congress party was on a roll. Its popularity was at a high after it won elections in eight provinces, among the eleven that went to the polls in the provincial elections of the winter of 1936–37 as mandated by the Government of India Act, 1935. The membership of the Congress had increased from 600,000 to 3,100,000 in the year leading to the Haripura Congress. Not only the crowds but the entire venue reflected the party's increasing clout, with the famous painter Nandalal Bose deployed to decorate the venue, which he did admirably.

Things could not have been better—a popular party with a popular president. Setting the tone, Bose in his presidential address enthusiastically said, 'the objective of the Congress is an independent and United India where no class and group or majority or minority may exploit one another to its own advantage and where all the elements in the nation may cooperate together for the common good and the advancement of the people of India.'

Noting that the Congress was going from strength to strength and was popular amongst all sections of society, Bose said that the principal problem in the country would be 'how to eradicate poverty.' He said that this would require a radical reform of the land system and abolition of feudalism. He also pointed out, 'a new industrial policy will have to be built up in place of the old one which has collapsed as result of mass production abroad and alien rule at home.' Bose added, 'A comprehensive scheme of industrial development under state ownership and state control will be indispensable.' He had thus clearly enunciated his economic philosophy.

During his long speech Bose referred to the stranglehold of the 'Central Government'. He cited figures for the budget for 1937–38 to show that out of the total expenditure of Rs 77.90 crore, the army got to spend Rs 44.61 crore, about 57 per cent of the expenditure of the central government. He also pointed out that the Central Legislative Assembly had by an overwhelming majority rejected this budget proposal. The Viceroy overwrote these objections using his powers.

Bose dwelt on many other subjects including the future of the Congress. He said that there was no question of the Congress party withering away after independence was attained. 'It will assume responsibility for administration and put through its programme for reconstruction,' he said. Addressing the apprehension in some quarters within the Congress that this could lead to a totalitarian regime Bose clarified that such a case would arise if a one-party situation arose like in Russia, Germany and Italy in that era. Bose said that India would be a multi-party polity and this would ensure that leaders were not thrust from the top but elected from the bottom.

Bose foresaw that the British would try to divide the country before leaving. He pointed out that the main feature of British imperialist policy in India was a policy of 'divide and rule' that set one community against another. He said, 'It is a well-known truism that every empire is based on a policy of divide and rule. But I doubt if any empire in the world has practiced this policy so skilfully, systematically and ruthlessly as Great Britain. In accordance with the policy, before power was handed over to the Irish people, Ulster was separated from the rest of Ireland. Similarly, before any power is handed over to the Palestinians, the Jews will be separated from the Arabs. An internal partition is necessary in order to neutralise the transference of power.' Netaji also felt that the changing nature of military technology would stem the unbridled power that the British once enjoyed. In his address at Haripura, Bose said, 'Today Britain can hardly call herself "the Mistress of the Seas". Her phenomenal rise in the 18th and 19th centuries was the result of her sea power. Her decline as an Empire in the 20th century will be the outcome of the emergence of a new factor in world history—Air Force.'

Bose also called for closer cooperation between the Congress party, its trade union arm and peasant organizations. He said that it was his personal opinion that these organizations should be affiliated to the Congress 'in order to bring all progressive and anti-imperialist organizations under the influence and control of the Congress.' He also pointed out that there had been 'a great deal of controversy over the question of forming a party, like the Congress Socialist Party, within the Congress. I hold no brief for the Congress Socialist Party and I am not a member of it. Nevertheless, I must say that I have been in agreement with its general principles and policies from the very beginning. It is desirable for the leftist elements to be consolidated into one party.' He was aware though that in large political groups such as the Congress there were also views that veered towards the right.

Bose touched upon a number of other matters in his speech. He said that the growing population of India was a cause of great worry. One of the most novel ideas he espoused was to promote a hybrid version of Hindi and Urdu as the national language of India. But there was a caveat: to make it easier to understand, the Roman script would be used. Bose had taken this idea from the Turkish leader Mustafa Kemal Atatürk who had introduced a similar system in his country.

The Congress president concluded his address with his vision for the tools to be deployed to gain freedom. 'I believe more than ever before that the method should be "satyagraha" or non-violent non-co-operation in the widest sense of the term, including civil disobedience. It would not be correct to call our method passive resistance. "Satyagraha", as I understand it is not merely passive resistance but active resistance as well, though that activity must be of a non-violent character,' Bose said. He added that non-violent non-cooperation would have to be restarted and the acceptance of office in the provinces as an experimental measure should not confine the party within the limits of strict constitutionalism in the future.

The presidency of the Congress in that era was largely ornamental and was passed on from one senior member to another senior member. The real power in the party was Mohandas Karamchand Gandhi and he ruled the roost. Congress members sought to be close to him so that they could share the glory. In fact there was a coterie of leaders around Gandhi. These included Rajendra Prasad, Sardar Vallabhbhai Patel and Bhulabhai Desai. Bose did not fall in this category—he was a leader in his own right. Even as Bose and Nehru were both part of the young radical group in the Congress party they were as different as chalk and cheese. Nehru owed his position in the Congress hierarchy quite a bit of the way to his father Motilal Nehru who had been one of the top leaders of the party in the 1920s. Jawaharlal was also fast becoming a key member of the Mahatma's coterie—that in later years transformed into the 'Congress High Command' (a term that was used to denote where power in the Congress lay).

As president of the Congress, Bose believed he had the right to chart an independent line, but in consultation with the supreme decision-making body in the party, the All India Congress Committee (AICC).

In line with this policy, Bose constituted the Planning Committee on 17 December 1938 which was to make a blueprint for the reconstruction of the country after independence. A forward looking idea, it was construed as a far reaching move by political analysts of the day. The party president invited Jawaharlal Nehru, who had been Congress president the two previous years, to chair the committee which included luminaries like scientist Meghnad Saha, engineer and architect Mokshagundam Visvesvaraya, and economist K.T. Shah. Incidentally in his presidential speech Bose had said, 'the State, on the advice of a Planning Commission, will have to adopt a comprehensive scheme for gradually socialising our entire agriculture and industrial system in the spheres of both production and distribution.' The choice of Nehru was significant—he had the favour of Gandhi and Bose felt that by letting Jawaharlal chair the Committee, it would have the acceptability of the Congress' supreme leader.

The coterie around the Mahatma had cast their votes in favour of Bose as president of the Congress for his sacrifices and his popularity among the masses. They would not have imagined that the Congress president had a mind of his own and that he would not fall in line and espouse the party line. Bose was clear in his views and was not about to change them to win favours from the coterie. He praised Gandhi but criticised policies that defined the Gandhian way. In fact the policy of radical transformation of the economy that he envisaged ran counter to the simplistic Gandhian model that assumed that all was good within a village, where every member lived in peace and harmony. Bose thought Gandhi was not only espousing backward ideas about village republics but was unwilling to recognise the different economic interests of landlords and peasants which led to underlying tensions. He realized that Gandhi in his battle for freedom was not willing to push hard for reforming the rural power structure. Gandhi's idea was to empower the Harijans by ensuring they stay within the Hindu fold. But Bose thought differently. He believed that a Hindu peasant and Muslim peasant had more in common than a Hindu landlord and a Hindu peasant. Bose's views leaned towards radical land reforms as a prerequisite for enabling the rural economy to grow. It was also essential to explain to the peasants where their economic interests lay. This understanding would allow them to steer clear of communal forces which focussed on unity of interests of homogeneous religious groups.

The young leader believed that independent India would be a federal India with a constitution that would include a declaration of rights and guarantee of civil liberties. Since he believed in no communal divisions on the basis of religion, or that of caste or class, in Bose's vision there would be a joint electorate in elections. This view was important in that era since the British were trying to divide Hindus and Muslims by promoting separate electorates for the two communities.

A researcher at Middlebury College in the UK ferreted out private correspondence from a number of archives in London for an academic paper that demonstrates that Bose had many reservations about Gandhi. Letters, quoted in Will Woodworth's study, 'The 1938–39 Clash of Mohandas Gandhi and Subhas Chandra Bose', says that Bose had lamented that the Congress party had begun to flounder since the Mahatma had transformed the Congress into a 'social service league'. Bose had also expressed that the 'two great limitations by Gandhi on (the) Congress programme were non-violence and non-interference in vested interests.' The letters were written to an activist A.R. Bhat who had helped Bose organize the Maharashtra Youth Conference in 1931. The letters also said: 'We must fall back on the support of the masses. The left wing of the Congress must immediately organize itself as an all-India party with socialist programme on (a) militant plan of action.' The letters must have been intercepted by intelligence agencies of that era since they were included in the records of the 'Public and Judicial (S) Department' archived in the British Library, London where they were accessed by Woodworth.

If the Gandhi coterie had elevated Bose to the presidency of the Congress for a year they soon realized that the young leader was mounting a challenge to the ideology espoused by the Mahatma. They alleged that Bose was baiting Gandhi. The immediate cause of the dispute was the successful provincial elections conducted under the provisions of the Government of India Act, 1935. The British rulers wanted to take it to its logical conclusion and hold elections for establishing a federal government. Bose was opposed to this since he felt that this was a British ploy for establishing nominal governance structures to be run by Indians but with little say. The real power would remain with the Viceroy who could exercise veto powers on major government decisions. Bose's view was that this was one way of stymieing the Independence movement: some moderates would be happy at the formation of governments with limited power and give up the fight for freedom. For Bose freedom meant throwing out the British out of the country, lock stock and barrel. Gandhi was also interested in this but did not come out so forcefully in the matter. Bose in fact did not even want the Congress to form the provincial governments. And now that they were in there trouble was already brewing. In the run-up to the Haripura Congress the prime ministers (the nomenclature used then, equivalent to chief ministers now) of the United Provinces and Bihar resigned over the refusal by the British Viceroy to sanction the release of political prisoners. This was an important point of agenda for the Congress party and subsequently the Viceroy agreed to allow the gradual release of political prisoners, with the provincial governments forwarding the requests to the provincial governors after evaluating them on a case-to-case basis.

Officially the Congress was still saying no to the federal government that the British were proposing but there was speculation that in the end the coterie that decided everything would fall for the plan. And that would be the end of the battle for full Independence. Such speculation was not unwarranted because even before the provincial elections, the bosses of the Congress party had said that the organization would not contest the elections but had later reversed their position.

Bose was so unhappy about this that on 9 July 1938 in his capacity as the president of the Congress he issued a statement warning against the adoption of the 'Federal Scheme' by the Congress. He said, 'I have no doubt in my mind that any effort to foist the Federal Scheme on the Congress will inevitably fail. If unfortunately it succeeds, it will break the Congress because I do not see how those who are conscientiously opposed to the Federal Scheme can take it lying down. Personally I think that any weakness shown by Congress or any section thereof during this fateful hour in India's history will amount to a treachery of the first magnitude to the cause of India's freedom.' It seems that Subhas Bose believed that sections of the Congress—and these were influential sections—were not only amenable to the federal government as proposed by the British but had decided amongst themselves on who would be ministers and which portfolios they would hold.

Subhas Chandra Bose realized that he would have to step in and offer his candidature for the post of President of the Congress party for a second term. Only this way he would be able to keep the British plan at bay. But there was an unwritten convention that a Congressman was the president only for one term. The Mahatma and his coterie decided upon the next candidate who would adorn the post. Needless to add, the Gandhi coterie was terribly upset when Bose put his hat into the ring for a second term. They realized that the young man challenged whatever Gandhi stood for and was thus a countervailing force. If he won, Gandhi's influence ran the risk of being severely eroded. If the Mahatma's importance was reduced, feared the coterie, where would they go? The coterie preferred that the Mahatma clear the appointment of the next party president as had almost become customary.

The original plan was to nominate Maulana Abul Kalam Azad for the position, but seeing the confusion and realizing that a contest was imminent, he withdrew. Bhogaraju Pattabhi Sitaramayya was now nominated as the new candidate for the presidency. It was made amply clear that Sitaramayya was Gandhi's candidate.

Bose was a consummate power player and he knew that the Gandhi group would try to marginalize him. He played up the election as a referendum on the federal scheme of government by the British. He argued that a vote for Sitaramayya would be a vote for moderation in Congress politics and for acceptance of the federal provisions of the Government of India Act, 1935. The moderates were on the backfoot: they asserted that they were as much as against the federal provisions as Bose and his followers. The moderates also claimed that they did not want to be part of an arrangement where they would technically be in power but in reality would be without any. But Bose had clearly struck a chord with Congress party members, and the Mahatma and his coterie were in a fix. They did not know how to counter the young leader. Gandhi now pitched an attack on the Indian princes who were oppressing their subjects. This was with an idea to change the focus.

In the end Bose won having polled 1,580 votes against the 1,375 polled by Sitaramayya. He released a statement thanking party members for the win from his hometown of Calcutta where he was awaiting the result. The coterie stood exposed, it was clear that they were not as formidable as was thought earlier, with Gandhi no longer the sole leader, popular though he might have remained.

But Gandhi with all the simplicity of his lifestyle and outer countenance was a master politician. He lamented from Wardha, where he lived, 'I was instrumental in inducing Dr Pattabhi not to withdraw his name when Maulana Saheb (Abul Kalam Azad) withdrew, this defeat is more mine than his... it is plain to me that the delegates do not approve of the principles and policy which I stand for. I rejoice in this defeat.' This statement was a masterstroke. Gandhi was enormously popular and a statement that he believed that his policy had been defeated was made to generate a wave of sympathy.

This was followed by a move that smacked of cheap politics more than anything else. Within a month, all the Congress Working Committee members resigned, save Bose and his elder brother Sarat Chandra Bose. The eleven members who resigned included members of the Mahatma's inner circle like Rajendra Prasad and Vallabhbhai Patel. The resigning members said that Bose was free to choose his own team. Bose pleaded with them, 'If only we sink our differences, pool all our resources and pull our full weight in the national struggle, we can make our attack on British imperialism irresistible.' He added (alluding to the World War that was imminent) that a rare opportunity presented itself to marginalise the imperialists and that it should not be missed.

On 7 March 1939 the Congress session opened at Tripuri near Jubbulpore. Now the Congress coterie played another masterstroke. They got one of their sympathisers, Govind Ballabh Pant (who was prime minister of United Provinces) to move a resolution that read, 'The Congress expresses its confidence in the work of the working committee which functioned during the last year and regrets that any aspersions should have been cast against any of its members. In view of the critical situation that may develop during the coming year (the looming war clouds) and in view of the fact that Mahatma Gandhi can alone lead the Congress and the country to a victory during such crisis, the Congress regards it as imperative that the Congress executive should command his implicit confidence and requests the President to appoint the working committee in accordance with the wishes of Gandhiji.'

The resolution was passed. Bose was now clearly cornered and had no option but to write to Mahatma Gandhi requesting him to nominate the working committee. But Gandhi did not oblige in spite of Bose writing to him multiple times. Instead Gandhi threw the ball back in Bose's court and asked him to nominate the working committee himself knowing full well that the All-India Congress Committee (AICC) resolution had empowered him to do so.

The next Congress meeting was close at hand and Bose realized that Gandhi and his acolytes were out to marginalise him. There was no way they would allow him to run the party. Bose resigned at the AICC meeting in Calcutta on 29 April recounting how it was now impossible for him to run the party and wondering whether the party could elect a new president. The Gandhi coterie was waiting for this opportunity. Rajendra Prasad, a key member of the Gandhi group was now chosen as the party president. The clique did not trust Bose and was bent upon keeping him down. A resolution of the Congress Working Committee banned Bose from holding any elective position in the Congress for three years. The coterie was wary that Subhas Bose could be elected as president of the Bengal Provincial Congress Committee which would empower him and give him political leverage. The ban was carried out in the name of maintaining party discipline. Bose had allegedly made some derogatory references to Congress leaders. Thus Bose was marginalised in the Congress party at a very crucial time. World War II broke out on 1 September 1939 with Germany invading Poland. This was a golden opportunity to put pressure on the British as Subhas Bose had earlier pointed out. But the coterie was only interested in perpetuating its own influence. It did not matter to them that they were cutting their nose to spite their face.

7

Escape from Calcutta

Four days after he was forced to quit as president of the Congress party, Subhas Chandra Bose formed the Forward Bloc. As the name suggested this would be a section of the Congress with progressive, forward looking ideas. In that way the Congress party was democratic—it allowed all manners of men with different ideologies to be in its fold, almost like an Indian joint family where all members found a place under the sun but only the patriarch called the shots. That is how the Congress Socialist Party too had existed in the fold of the Congress. The idea was to spread the ideology of the Congress across a broad spectrum (even as leadership of the party was confined to a coterie). The formal announcement of the Forward Bloc was made at a rally at Calcutta on 3 May 1939 and Bose got the members to pledge that they would never 'turn their back to the British' and resolutely face the colonial rulers. They signed the pledge with their own blood. Out of his leadership position, Bose hoped that the Forward Bloc would develop an alternative leadership in the Congress by rallying left-wing forces and moved quickly, holding a conference in Bombay at the end of June. Thereafter Bose started travelling across the country to popularise the Forward Bloc. He was also busy organizing various conferences: the Anti-Imperialist Conference held at Nagpur in October 1939, the All India Students' Conference held at Delhi in January 1940 and the Anti-Compromise Conference held at Ramgarh in March 1940.

The Forward Bloc held its first all India conference in Nagpur between 20–22 June 1940 and now Subhas Bose seemed to have decided that the organization would be a separate political party with a socialist orientation. To keep up the tempo of opposition to the British, Bose announced a march to the Holwell Monument in Calcutta on 3 July 1940. This edifice had been erected by the British to commemorate the Black Hole tragedy of 1756 that occurred in the aftermath of the sacking of Fort William, the headquarters of the East India Company in Calcutta, by the Nawab of Bengal, Siraj ud-Daulah. Since the East India Company was not obeying his dictates, Siraj marched from his capital in Murshidabad and threw the English out of Calcutta. The story goes that a number of prisoners were locked up in a small room overnight. According to John Zephaniah Holwell, a prisoner, 123 of the 146 prisoners died because the room was too small to accommodate everybody. But the common belief was that the incident was highly exaggerated. Holwell's claim provided the perfect ruse for the Company to attack Siraj a year later and take over the administration of Bengal. This was the beginning of the English conquest of India. Bose declared that the Holwell Monument was a symbol of colonialism and should be demolished.

The British government was now very alarmed. They had always been very cautious about Bose. They knew he was not like Gandhi and his coterie who were more amenable to the British point of view. When Bose was forced out of the Congress, they had rejoiced. He would be out on a limb, they had reasoned. But Bose showed no signs of relenting. With the establishment of the Forward Bloc he was back in political action. In fact Bose was focussing on Bengal—possibly because he had the greatest strength in this province—and was showing signs of becoming a bigger headache than ever before for the colonial powers. With World War II now in full swing, the British decided to invoke sections of the draconian Defence of India Act, 1939, that gave the

Viceroy wide powers to ensure the defence of British India. Bose was arrested under the provisions of this Act on 2 July 1940 and could expect to remain in jail for an indefinite period, although this was not stated explicitly.

Bose understood though that the country's colonial rulers would not let him off till the War ended. They would not want him out creating problems for them in the midst of the raging conflict. Even before being incarcerated he had been planning to seek the support of foreign powers to free India from the British yoke. He had thought of Japan, a rising Asian power. Being Asian he thought the Japanese would have more empathy for the Indian cause. The Japanese vice foreign minister had visited Calcutta in 1938 and had met Bose confidentially at the house of a third person. Thus Bose knew that the Japanese would not be hostile to his efforts. He immediately despatched Lala Shankar Lal, who had served as general secretary of the Forward Bloc for a year, to Japan. Shankar Lal's brief was to talk to Japanese officials and assess whether Bose could move to Japan and whether the Japanese would help in his quest for India's freedom. Shankar Lal called on the Japanese foreign minister and also the German, Italian and Russian ambassadors in Tokyo.

By the time Shankar Lal returned to India, Bose was already in jail. Since non-family members were not allowed to meet him, Shankar Lal had to send a coded message through Bose's nephew who entered the jail masquerading as an electrician. 'All friends are happy and well and are anxious and waiting to welcome you. We see no reason for you to be where you are, when there is so much to be done outside.' Bose understood the import of Shankar Lal's confabulations with the Japanese. Since breaking out of the jail was not a logical option, he devised a brilliant plan to force the British to release him. Why not go on hunger strike? That way his health, which was not so good anyway, would deteriorate and the British administrators would be forced to release him.

He now wrote a letter to the government: 'Government is determined to hold me in prison by brute force. I say in reply: Release me or I shall refuse to live and it is for me whether I choose to live or die. The individual may die so that the nation may live. Today I must die, so that India may live, win freedom and glory.' On 29 November 1940, after writing this letter, Bose embarked on the hunger strike. He drank water with a little salt everyday and his fragile health began to deteriorate. The government panicked: if anything happened to him, all hell would break loose. On 2 December 1940 the British government decided that they would release Bose if his health deteriorated any further. They also contemplated force-feeding him but Bose warned his jailers against trying this tactic to bring him to heel. On 5 December 1940 the government finally decided to release their prisoner as doctors recommended that incarcerating him further would be risky. It was decided that he would be put under house arrest in his family home at Elgin Road in Calcutta. They had also made up their mind that once their prisoner regained his health he would be sent back to jail. Bose was carried out of jail on a stretcher, put on an ambulance and sent back home.

A new plan was brewing in the mind of the leader—something that the British knew nothing of, even as they had an inkling that he had been in touch with the Japanese. Bose's plans to seek international help to free India were now directed at another country. Why not go to the Soviet Union and seek the help of Joseph Stalin to free India? The Soviet Union offered an alternative model of development—a socialist one—which was preferable to a capitalist model. In his mind, Bose was sure that the Russians would help, if only he could reach Soviet territory. He could possibly reach the Soviet Union through Afghanistan using the land route. He remembered his trusted associate, Mian Akbar Shah, who headed the Forward Bloc in the North-West Frontier Province (NWFP). A telegram was promptly relayed to Akbar Shah in his village in Nowshera district. It read: 'Reach Calcutta—Bose.'

Without any delay Akbar Shah took the Frontier Mail from

Peshawar and reached Howrah after three days of travelling, changing his train en route at Delhi. After checking in to a hotel in Calcutta, he went to see his leader. Bose was in bed, weak and ushaven. The leader came to the point quickly: 'I want to go abroad through the tribal territories of Kabul. The War is on and I must get out of India and seek the help of leaders of countries which are enemies of British Imperialism and seek their help. The Soviet government is one of them. I need your help.' Shah who had full faith in his leader's prowess agreed to help. 'It is not a difficult task. You have to travel to Peshawar by train and through the tribal territories in disguise,' said Shah.

Plans were quickly finalised. Subhas Bose would grow a full beard and disguise himself as a Muslim by the name of Ziauddin. He would pose as a roving insurance agent.

Sisir Bose, a favourite nephew of Netaji, then twenty years old was roped into the plan. Shah and Sisir went to a shop selling items required for Bose's disguise—Wachel Molla's—on Dharmatala Street. Shah told his leader that he would like him to cover his mouth and ears when passing through the tribal areas. But that would be later. Even as he was planning an exit, Subhas kept up the tempo of political work, corresponding with Mahatma Gandhi on important political matters and also with leaders like Jaya Prakash Narayan.

On 16 January 1941 Subhas Bose told his family members that he would like to go into seclusion to pray and meditate and that he should not be disturbed in his retreat. The bedroom was partitioned with a small aperture for serving food. Nobody suspected anything because Bose had a spiritual streak in him and this was well known. In fact at the age of sixteen, as a college student, he had disappeared for a year on a pilgrimage to places like Mathura, Vrindavan, Benares (Varanasi) and Haridwar—merely informing his guardians through a postcard that he was travelling. In *An Indian Pilgrim: An Unfinished Autobiography* Subhas has written about his thirst to find a guru (spiritual teacher). He writes of Sri Ramakrishna and Swami Vivekananda's influence, and their teaching that there could be no realisation without renunciation.

Late at night, either on 16 or 17 January 1941, Bose tiptoed down the rear staircase of the house to a car parked on the driveway disguised as a Pathan in a closed-collar brown long coat, broad pyjamas and a black fez. His two nephews Sisir and Aurobindo were with him. Sisir was to drive him down to Gomoh, 240 km away in Bihar where he would board the Howrah–Kalka Mail. Bose did not want to risk taking the train from the crowded Howrah station because he could well be identified in spite of his disguise. Gomoh was a wayside railway station with hardly any traffic. Moreover he would board the train there in the dead of night.

Bose opened the car door and sat on the rear seat. He placed his holdall on the front seat. Sisir Bose opened the gate of the house and drove out with a sputtering noise. This was deliberate since he did not want to give an impression that the car was sneaking out. Some of the sleuths from the Criminal Investigation Department (CID) tasked to keep watch on him were sleeping on a wooden cot. Being the middle of January it was quite cold and the irritated CID men roused from their slumber merely looked at the car before going back to sleep. They thought that this car—a German made 'Wanderer' owned by Sarat Bose bearing the licence number BLA 7169—was returning to his residence at Woodburn Park close by.

The car exited North Calcutta and drove out through the Barrackpore Trunk Road and on to the Grand Trunk Road that still connects eastern India to the north. Driving through the night they reached Burari near Dhanbad in Bihar where another nephew worked as a coal mine manager. To maintain secrecy, Bose arrived alone in the morning at his nephew's house posing as an insurance agent. The nephew was going out to work and asked Bose to wait till lunch time. At lunch Subhas, still posing as an insurance agent asked his nephew if he could wait till evening when he had a train to catch. This request was granted. In all probability, the nephew knew whom he was hosting, but the duo continued their role play to ensure that the suspicion of servants was not aroused. The servants and also some distant relatives in the Bose household in Calcutta were also CID informants and it was necessary to be careful.

A little past midnight of 18 January Bose boarded the Howrah–Kalka Mail at Gomoh. Sisir and Aurobindo Bose left him a little distance away from the station and watched as their uncle melted away in the distance. This was the last time they were to see him.

Changing trains in Delhi, Bose now perfectly looking the part of Ziauddin, travelling insurance agent based out of Civil Lines, Jubbulpore, reached Peshawar on the evening of 21 January 1941. He was received by Akbar Shah and put up at the budget Taj Mahal Hotel in the middle of the city. Next morning he was moved to a rented house in the Kabuli Gate area of the city and introduced to Bhagat Ram Talwar who would be his guide through the tribal territories and also to Abid Shah who would drive them out of Peshawar.

On the morning of 22 January, Abid Shah drove by in his 1932 model Chevrolet with Talwar and was joined by Bose, who had now decided to act deaf and dumb. This was because he did not understand any local language. Bose was now dressed in an old Pathani outfit. Subhas and Talwar alighted at the outskirts of the village Pishkam Maina, while Abid Shah turned back. Talwar had assumed the name of Rahmat Khan for the journey. He lived in the area and was familiar with the local customs and practices. He posed as Subhas' uncle who looked every inch the Pathan with his good physique, sharp features and fair complexion. Both of them trudged to the village *serai* (inn) and took shelter there overnight along with twenty-five other travellers. The next morning—23 January—on Subhas' birthday they began the long trek to the Afghan border. Bose was unused to these high altitudes and the rough terrain and was almost out of breath. At some places they hired a mule. Their progress was slow but Bose was determined and the duo crossed some mountain passes in the buffer zone of the tribal areas that lay between India and Afghanistan. Being January, some of the mountain passes were still covered with snow. In the end they took two days to cross a distance that could have taken a few hours by car on the main road. This was a risk that Bose could ill-afford because of all the outposts manned by police. Once they crossed the Durand Line into Afghanistan in the morning, the duo came onto the main road to Jalalabad. They stopped a truck and requested a ride. Past lunch-time they entered Kabul through the Lahori Gate. It was 31 January. Kabul in those days was just an overgrown village with a few concrete houses and the duo took refuge in a local *serai*.

Meanwhile in Calcutta all hell had broken loose at the Elgin Road residence after it was discovered that Bose had fled. This was also part of a pre-arranged plan to confuse the British. Bose had taken a nephew and niece into confidence. The nephew used to eat the food sent into Bose's room every day but on 26 January the niece 'discovered' that her uncle was nowhere to be found. The news was leaked through the sympathetic *Ananda Bazar Patrika* and the *Hindustan Standard*. Bose had written some post-dated letters before he had left and these had been posted to give the impression that he was still around. The British knew that the man under watch had given them the slip though they did not know where he was headed. They speculated that he had boarded a ship and was on the way to Japan via Penang, Singapore and Hong Kong based on intelligence reports of his connection with the Japanese. They did not realize that Bose had gone the other way and crossed over the Indian border (or was on the way to do so). In fact they never thought of looking for Bose in Peshawar or beyond. On their part, the Bose family started to propagate rumours that he had probably renounced the world and gone away to become an ascetic. The British Indian police was initially confused by these rumours but reasoned that such an assessment would be wrong: if Bose had disappeared it would only be to further the cause of India's freedom.

Though a ramshackle town, Kabul was teeming with spies and agents of various countries in those days. That was but natural because the Afghan capital allowed access to both Europe and Soviet Russia. A great game was being played out here. The Italians, Germans and the Soviet Union all had their representatives in the city. But this did not make Bose's task any easier. The Soviets were reluctant to offer any refuge to him: this was natural. The country was expecting an attack by Germany. This would mean that the Soviet Union would have to treat the British as an ally and in that situation the Russians did not want to harbour an enemy of London. These apprehensions would prove correct, because on 22 June 1941, the Germans invaded Soviet Russia. Bose was rather disheartened at the Soviet position because his first preference for assistance had been Moscow. After waiting for a few days and making no headway Bose barged into the German embassy in Kabul and sought their help. Even as the Germans sought time to seek instructions from headquarters they asked Bose not to be rash and fall foul of the Afghan security apparatus.

The Italian Legation in Kabul proved more helpful—Bose was directed to them by the Germans themselves who were ready to receive him in Berlin. A meeting with the chief of the Italian Legation was fixed on the evening of 22 February and it turned out to be a great success. The Italians provided Bose with an Italian passport in the name of Orlando Mazzotta. Bose was ready to leave. There were two ways to reach Europe: one was through Iran, Iraq and Turkey, the other way was to go through Soviet territory. The Italians and Germans pleaded with the Soviet Union to issue Bose a transit visa through their country. Moscow held off on issuing a travel document to Bose, even though the German ambassador in Moscow personally intervened in the matter. At Bose's end, his residency at the *serai* was becoming untenable, with the suspicions of some sections of the Afghan police having been aroused. A particular Afghan policeman had to be bribed twice: once with cash and then with a favourite wristwatch, gifted to Bose by his father. It was not deemed suitable for Bose to remain in the *serai* for too long. Bhagat Ram approached an acquaintance of his, Uttam Chand Malhotra, a trader in Kabul for help. Bose took refuge in the home of Uttam Chand in the Indian quarters of Kabul. It was felt that he would be safer if he remained in the company of Indians.

While Bose waited for his travel plans to coalesce he began penning a tract on the country's political scenario. He wrote that the need of the hour was a leftist antithesis to the rightist thesis that held sway in Indian politics. He argued that Gandhi in the early 1920s had also been an antithesis to the status quo but had later changed. He asserted that the Forward Bloc had helped the Congress back onto the path of struggle, stimulated the party, and helped lift it back from stagnation. While leaving Kabul, Bose passed on the manuscript to Bhagat Ram with a request that he should go to Calcutta and hand it over to Sarat Chandra Bose. The manuscript was given a post-date and marked—'Written from somewhere in Europe.' Subhas Bose finally exited Kabul at dawn on 18 March—in a car provided by the Italians—the last two days of his extended stay in Kabul had been spent at the home of an Italian diplomat. Bose boarded a train a little later and reached Moscow via Samarkand. From Moscow he flew into Berlin. The date was 2 April 1941.

8

In Hitler's Germany

On 3 April 1941 a day after he landed in Berlin, Subhas Chandra Bose arrived at the German foreign office on Wilhelmstrasse where he was received by the under-secretary of state, Ernst Woermann. Bose got to the point of his visit without delay. He said that he wanted to liberate India from British suzerainty and requested German help for this cause. He told his interlocutor that as a prelude to further assistance they could recognise a provisional government of India-in-exile that would be set up. Bose went on to make a detailed presentation of his plans. Woermann was struck by the well worked out plans but was too amazed to respond. While remaining more or less silent, he possibly realized that what Bose wanted, ran counter to the ideas of the Führer.

Adolf Hitler thought very poorly of India and saw the Indian freedom movement as a rebellion of the inferior Hindu race against the valorous Anglo-Nordics. The latter, in Hitler's world view, were the only ones who had the right to dominate the world. In *Mein Kampf*, Hitler had written, 'Quite aside from the fact that I as a man of Germanic blood, would, in spite of everything rather see India under English rule than any other.'

At one level, for Hitler, World War II was a battle for colonies. After its World War I defeat, Germany had lost both prestige and colonies.

The reparations imposed on the country had deeply affected the German psyche which was used to seeing itself as a superior people. The rise of Hitler was linked to the German quest for restoration of prestige. Hitler himself was a colonialist and his battle with the British was for the redistribution of colonies. Hitler was quite content to leave India to Britain and to see the continuation of the British Empire if only Germany was given a free hand in Eastern Europe and Russia. 'The land for us and the sea for them' (meaning Britain) was Hitler's motto. It was the Führer's deepest desire to see Russia as a colony of Germany as India was of Great Britain's.

Having had a long sojourn in Europe a few years earlier recuperating from his health problems, Bose was not totally ignorant of what Hitler stood for. In fact Hitler's comments about India in *Mein Kampf* had come to Bose's notice in February 1933 when he was in Berlin. He had sought an audience with the German leader intending to urge him to revise his views on India. The meeting never materialized and Bose could only meet the mayor of Berlin. In 1936 when Hitler referred to white superiority in a speech, a livid Bose held a press conference in Geneva denouncing Hitler and advocated a trade boycott of Germany.

Yet, Bose pushed ahead with his plans to seek assistance from the Germans. He was totally consumed by his desire to see India free and was prepared to go to any length and take the help of anyone who could be of assistance in this matter. In fact this was the guiding principle of his life and Bose was buoyed by the early successes of the Germans during the War, which encouraged him to seek their assistance.

Woermann did not throw out Bose's request and did not apprise him on Hitler's world view, especially those on Russia. Instead he said that he would brief his bosses on the Indian leader's plans. Bose himself promised to get back with a detailed plan in writing. A few days later, on 9 April, Bose put forth a detailed proposal that suggested that the Axis powers would sign a treaty with the Free India government-in-exile, guaranteeing India's independence once World War II was won. He also proposed that an army consisting of 50,000 Indian soldiers could be established with recruits from prisoners of war taken by the Axis powers. Many British Indian troops had already been taken prisoner in North Africa. There was also a provision that after liberating India, Germany would hand over governance responsibilities to the government-in-exile headed by Bose.

The German leadership was impressed by the confidence and resolution shown by Bose, which prompted them to allow him into Berlin in the first place. But they were unable to agree to his proposal. Linking India's liberation with the War would imply that one of the reasons it was being fought was to free India. This reluctance to agree with the conditions set by Bose was not communicated to him straight away. Again, time was sought from him and Woermann indicated to Bose that the Germans were going out of the way to accommodate his needs.

True to his nature, Bose would not allow this latest obstruction to demoralize him. Consumed by the passion to free India, Bose was back at the German foreign office a month later—on 13 May—with a draft declaration of India's independence. The declaration envisioned that the people of India would themselves decide on their future Constitution after liberation of the country and that Germany should accept this absolute right. Germany would also take full responsibility to liberate India and would recognise the government of independent India. Even as there was nothing substantial in the proposal for the Germans, it was drafted in the expectation that the Germans would help India in return for the satisfaction of seeing their prime enemy, the British diminished.

The Germans had now begun to be wary about Bose: he was becoming too demanding a man, they thought. They had seen him as a refugee, or a leader in refuge whom they could use to their advantage whenever required. But this man was turning out to be different. On 24 May, the German foreign office got back to Bose. They suggested that a Free India Centre in Berlin should be set up. A loan of 10 million Reich Marks for the purpose was approved with 12,000 RMs set aside for the personal expenses of Bose. To figure out what he was up to, Bose was put on surveillance, his phone tapped and correspondence opened. Bose was not aware of this although he may have suspected.

Prior to this, Bose was in Rome on 5 May to reconnect with the Italian leaders, the country being aligned with the Axis powers. Bose had kept connections with the Italian leaders all through his sojourn in Europe in the early 1930s. He was hopeful of being received well because it was the Italians who had taken the lead in getting him out of Kabul. In Rome, Bose met the Italian foreign minister, Galeazzo Ciano and discussed the draft declaration of India's independence. In turn, Ciano, the son-in-law of Benito Mussolini took Bose over to meet the Duce. The Italian leader was willing to help but Italy's power had weakened by then and there was no question of taking an individual stand without German concurrence. Mussolini politely told Bose that he should discuss the matter with the Germans and convince them to assist him.

On 22 June 1941 Germany invaded the Soviet Union and Bose realized that any assistance from the Germans would be counterproductive. In India the Soviet Union was held in great esteem with the Communist model of governance looked at with approval by the intelligentsia. By implication a Germany that had invaded the Soviet Union would be seen in poor light by Indians. So if the Germans came forward to liberate India this would be taken with some scepticism by the Indians. This was especially so because Indian leaders like Mahatma Gandhi and Jawaharlal Nehru were critical of the Nazi regime.

Bose promptly decried the German attack on Russia in a letter written to German foreign minister, Joachim von Ribbentrop in August 1941. Bose expressed his fear that this action would put a spanner in the works to the evolving plans of German intervention in liberating India. Bose also sought an appointment with the foreign minister and met him for the second time in a year in November 1941.

In an earlier meeting at the end of April, Bose had sought a status quo in German policy towards the Russians till the British were totally cleared from North Africa. This meeting had helped establish good chemistry between Ribbentrop and Bose, if for nothing else, based on their mutual hatred of the British. Ribbentrop, who had been ambassador to London, thought rather poorly of the British.

At the November meeting Bose again made a demand that the Germans recognise independence for India. He also asked that the objectionable observations about Indians in Hitler's *Mein Kampf* be expunged. Nothing substantial seems to have come out of the meeting, although the foreign minister promised to look into Netaji's demands. Ribbentrop apparently told Bose that the guiding principle of German policy was not to promise anything which could not be carried out later. In other words the Germans were doubtful if they would ultimately launch an offensive to free India.

Bose also made a request for a meeting with Hitler. This time, he was given an audience, though he had to wait for many months. The meeting took place on 29 May 1942 at the Reich Chancellery.

The meeting appears to have been disastrous. Besides Ribbentrop other German ministers were also present. Hitler who was at the zenith of his power was at his boastful best and as soon as Bose arrived he launched into a long lecture on world politics. Bose was hardly enjoying this although civility demanded that he keep quiet. Hitler was very dismissive about India and boasted that if the Germans were to conquer India they would only take a year or two to spread their influence across the country. If Indians were to take charge of India it would take them 100–200 years to put their house in order. He seems to have been briefed on the Indian political situation and said that Nehru's anti-fascist and anti-Nazi approach would come to naught and at the same time brushed away Gandhi's policy of passive resistance as ineffective. Hitler made no secret of his expansionist designs and condescended to invite Bose to join the Nazis in triggering India's liberation. At the end of the meeting a slightly miffed Bose (on wrongly interpreting a statement by Hitler) told his interpreter Adam von Trot to tell the Führer, 'Your

Excellency, I have been in politics all my life and I do not need any advice from anyone.' Bose also requested Hitler to expunge adverse reactions about India from his *Mein Kampf*. This does not seem to have had any impact on the German leader who merely mentioned that these opinions were of the past.

Whatever illusions Bose might have had about the Germans were now broken. In fact as he waited in Berlin indefinitely, Bose was getting very restive. He had come to Germany hopeful of assistance to fight against the common enemy—the British. But now it was clear to Bose that nothing more could be achieved by staying put in Berlin. He also realized that the only reason that Hitler had for supporting him had little to do with the independence of India. Hitler wanted to use India as a bargaining chip in his battle against Great Britain—if he could corner the British on India then they would be compelled to exit from the War in Europe and allow him a free hand.

Bose now expressed a desire to quit Berlin. Even though Hitler had behaved in a condescending manner towards Bose he and also ministers like Ribbentrop had been impressed by Bose's courage and leadership qualities. For Hitler and his followers, who habitually disapproved of people or ideas that did not match their view, to be impressed with someone was really significant.

Though Bose's mission in Berlin had been a failure, in some ways it had resulted in gains. The Indian Legion (Indische Legion), initiated by Bose after his arrival in Germany in 1941, was raised from among Indian prisoners of war and expatriates. Bose was to create a volunteer base of 10,000, which would go ahead of the German forces to invade India through Russia, Persia and Afghanistan. Bose visited different camps that housed Indian prisoners of wars of the British Indian Army and exhorted them to join the force that he was raising to liberate India. In most places he got encouraging responses although there were refusals as well. The soldiers had taken an oath to serve the British Army and were not willing to switch over to the German side, especially after the reports they had heard of the atrocities committed by the Nazis. Eventually a fighting force of 3,000 was raised. Netaji was able to convince the Germans that the force would only be used to liberate India. At one stage when the force was sought to be deployed in Greece, Bose had protested and got the move rescinded.

Bose went about building the Indian Legion with utter seriousness. In Berlin in those days there were similar groups like the Cossack Legion, Turkish Legion and the Georgian Legion. These were formed by people from these regions whose countries had been swallowed by the Russians into the massive Soviet Union. But these groups did not exhibit the energy and organization that the Indian Legion came to be known for under the leadership of Bose. Its emblem, the springing tiger, aptly described what Bose wanted the body to do. It was the members of the Legion who began addressing Bose with the honorific Netaji, the epithet by which he has been immortalized. The salutation 'Jai Hind', so commonly used in India now, especially in the modern Indian Armed Forces has its origin in the Indian Legion. It is the shortened version of 'Jai Hindustan Ki' which was framed by Netaji's secretary Abid Hasan Safrani as the Legion's battle cry. It was Bose who shortened it to Jai Hind. There is an interesting anecdote about the slogan—apparently Safrani heard two Rajput soldiers wishing each other Jai Ramji Ki and conjured the slogan Jai Hindustan Ki.

The Indian Legion, on the approval of Netaji, also adopted *Jana Gana Mana* as its anthem—to be adopted as the national anthem of the country after Independence. It was sung by the Legion for the first time on 11 September 1942, on the occasion of the foundation of the Indo–German society.

The British Indian Army was organized on racial lines, the regiments raised on the basis of caste and community. Netaji understood that the force he was raising should be above caste and creed. He insisted that the units being raised must have a mix of men from different regions, castes and communities. A radical move, there were Rajputs with Marathas, Hindus with Muslims and Sikhs serving side-by-side.

Probably the most daring action by the Indian Legion was *Operation*

Bajadere which was launched in January 1942. Here, a contingent of a hundred highly efficient and trained soldiers (trained by the Brandenburgers—German special forces) were para-dropped into parts of Baluchistan that were being held by Persia. Their mission was to infiltrate into British India and foment trouble against the rulers. History does not record whether they were successful in their efforts.

The story of Netaji's stay in Germany cannot be completed without reference to the Azad Hind Radio that was established in Berlin. It was a propaganda radio station established to keep the morale of the freedom fighters high. The station broadcast weekly bulletins in various Indian languages like Hindi, Bengali, Tamil, Marathi, Punjabi, Pashto, and Urdu. Bose would himself broadcast messages from time to time and share his perspectives on contemporary events. The Azad Hind Radio began broadcasting from 19 January 1942 with the avowed objective of presenting world affairs from a purely nationalistic viewpoint and shorn of British propaganda. Netaji termed the British Broadcasting Corporation or the BBC as Bluff and Bluster Corporation. He said that the British broadcaster was the only choice for the Indian public to hook into international information and thus they were unconsciously imbibing British propaganda.

On 28 February 1942, after the fall of Singapore to the Japanese, an exuberant Netaji went on air announcing that the fall meant that the collapse of the British Empire was imminent and the iniquitous regime that it symbolised would end. Bose announced that it signified the dawn of a new era in Indian history. 'The hour of India's salvation is at hand, India will now rise and break the chains of servitude that have bound her so long.'

Netaji went on air again on 20 July 1942. This was after the declaration of Egyptian independence by the Axis powers. He said, 'The British Empire has two lungs—Egypt and India. Without Egypt, the Empire would be reduced to one lung. If the other lung is also put out of action death will immediately follow.'

With the fall of Singapore to the Japanese, Netaji's desire to leave

Berlin and move to the Far Eastern front intensified. With the Japanese knocking at the doorsteps of India, Netaji wanted to join them. However, Bose did not want to leave Germany before he had met Hitler, which took place at the end of May. After this fateful meeting Netaji wrote to Ribbentrop in July of his desire to go over to Asia urgently. The Germans had no objection with this move but a prolonged discussion ensued on the *modus operandi* to move him to the distant continent in the midst of the War. One of the options discussed was to fly him out on an Italian plane taking off from somewhere in that country. In fact, in November, Bose journeyed to Italy to catch a plane. But the idea of flying out the Indian leader was finally given up upon Hitler's orders who said that the Indian leader was too important a person to allow his life to be risked in such a manner. There were chances that his aircraft would be shot down by the Allied Forces. It was then that the plan for transporting him in a submarine came up: the initial idea was to take him to the French coast (France was then under German occupation) where he would board a Japanese I-10 submarine onwards to Asia. By the time the detailed plans were finalised the sea off the island of Madagascar in the Indian Ocean was zeroed upon as the place where the Japanese would pick him up. The Germans would transfer Netaji to Madagascar in their own submarine. Initially it seems the Japanese imperial navy had reservations about allowing Netaji into their submarine: their regulations prohibited carrying civilians. Only when they were told that Bose was no civilian but the commander-in-chief of the India's liberation army did they relent.

In preparation for his submarine journey Netaji left Berlin by train for Kiel accompanied by his secretary Abid Hasan Safrani. Netaji's plans were kept top secret and even Safrani did not know where they were headed. Bose and Safrani went down into the cramped but brand new U-180 submarine on 8 February 1943 and were welcomed by Captain Werner Musemberg. When Netaji went down in the submarine he bid adieu to his wife with whom he had spent time together in Berlin. In fact, he would never see her again. Bose's German sojourn had allowed him conjugal bliss. He had met his wife Emilie Schenkl a few years previously while he was recuperating in Vienna and simultaneously writing his Indian memoirs. Emilie—who was almost fourteen years younger than Bose—was engaged by the leader because she was good at taking short hand and typing.

Anybody who has been into a submarine knows how claustrophobic life can be in such a vessel. There is hardly any room to move around and the lack of natural light for a prolonged period can affect the psyche of anyone but a trained submariner. But Netaji would have undergone any hardship for the sake of India's freedom. As the submarine slunk up the Norwegian coast and slid into the Atlantic, Bose was putting the confinement to good use. He busied himself dictating future speeches to Hasan to help clarify his thoughts. The notes were only for the purpose of future preparedness. Bose never spoke from written speeches—his delivery was always extempore. Otherwise, it was a tough life—the smell of diesel and sweat of mariners compounded by lack of any proper food that would suit the Indian palate. There was a close call once when the submarine surfaced to breathe and brushed across a British tanker, *Corbis* that was sailing straight towards it. The submarine jerked and there was panic all through. But Netaji was unperturbed. He went on with his dictation and even chided Hasan for not paying full attention to what he was saying. For the record, the German submarine sank the tanker. It seems that the Indian leader used to get radio messages on board the submarine, which kept him abreast of the war situation.

Sailing past West Africa, around the tip of Africa, the submarine entered the Indian Ocean. On 26 April 1943, over two and a half months since the U-boat set sail from its home base, the German and Japanese submarines sighted each other. But the weather was inclement and the seas were rough. It took more than a day to manoeuvre the transfer of Bose and Safrani from one submarine to the other. Tied with a rope and afloat on a rubber dinghy that bobbed from side to side, a drenched Netaji along with his aide made it into the Japanese submarine and were welcomed by Captain Masao Teraoka and Lieutenant Commander Izu Juichi. The Japanese submarine I-10 was a little roomier and a little over ten days later Netaji disembarked at Sabang, a group of islands off Sumatra.

It was good that Netaji took a decision to shift to South-east Asia when he did. As Netaji embarked on his voyage, the Germans lost the Battle of Stalingrad and the German commander surrendered to Soviet forces on 2 February 1943. This was a decisive battle that turned the tide against the Germans. With the Soviets victorious—albeit with sizeable casualties—it would no longer be possible for German forces to march to India.

9

INA and Azad Hind Government

The story of Subhas Chandra Bose and the Indian National Army (INA) begins with another Bose. No relative of Subhas Chandra, Rashbehari Bose was a revolutionary involved with the Ghadar Party and shot to fame because he was part of the group that threw a bomb at Lord Charles Hardinge who was Viceroy of India from 1910–16. On 23 December 1912, when a procession to celebrate the shifting of the capital of India from Calcutta to Delhi passed through the Chandni Chowk area in the new capital, one of the members of the group threw a bomb at the Viceroy who was mounted on an elephant. He was injured and before long a manhunt to nab the culprits was underway. Although the others involved were caught and later hanged, Rashbehari managed to dodge the police and escaped to Japan on a ship headed to that country, using a false identity. He lived underground in Japan for many years as the British discovered his whereabouts and pressed for his extradition—though unsuccessfully. He later married a Japanese lady and became a citizen in 1923. He is credited for having introduced Indian curry in Japan and even held a patent for the dish. Over the years, he became committed to the Japanese cause and a trusted advisor on Indian matters. When the Japanese overran Kuala Lumpur on 11 January 1942 and Singapore on 15 February 1942, and began planning to move against the British in India they looked towards Rashbehari for making this possible.

Rashbehari took up the cue and convened a conference in Tokyo from 28–30 March to discuss matters relating to India. It was decided that an Indian Independence League would be instituted to give an impetus to the Indian freedom movement in East Asia. Rashbehari was appointed the head of the League and resolved military action against India through a national army comprising Indians and under Indian command. After the fall of Singapore some 12,000 Indian prisoners of war (POW) were transferred to the command of Captain Mohan Singh (also a POW) for raising the INA, which was formally proclaimed in April that year. Rashbehari too came to Singapore to discuss with Mohan Singh and the Japanese army commanders on how the military action would be carried out.

By the middle of June 1942 all plans were finalised at a conference in Bangkok which reaffirmed Rashbehari Bose as the chairman of the Council of Action of the League, and the INA led by Mohan Singh subordinate to it. The headquarters of the Council were to be established in Singapore.

However, within a few months the INA came apart with serious differences cropping up between Rashbehari Bose and Mohan Singh. In November it was disbanded as Singh and his associates rose in rebellion against the leadership style of Rashbehari. The soldiers felt that Rashbehari was giving primacy to Japanese interests. Singh was subsequently put under arrest by the Japanese. The INA was however revived a few months later in February 1943 under Lieutenant Colonel Jagannathrao Krishnarao Bhonsle, also a POW. The need for Netaji was never more acutely felt among the Indian community in Singapore. They had all heard of his exploits in Germany and many INA soldiers said that they would be willing to continue if Bose took charge. The Japanese, who for long had put their trust in Rashbehari, began to feel that Netaji would be a better person to lead the Indian war effort.

On arriving at the Sumatran islet in May 1943, Bose was received by Colonel Yamamoto Bin, president of the Hikari Kikan, the group set up by the Japanese to liaise with India. Soon thereafter Netaji, accompanied by Yamamoto, left for Tokyo by air, stopping en route at Penang, Manila, Saigon and Taiwan. The two landed in Tokyo on 16 May, Netaji going incognito by the name Matsuda. From the next day onwards Netaji began his meetings with important people in government, including the chiefs of staff of the army, navy, the navy minister and the foreign minister, in the Japanese capital. A meeting with the Japanese prime minister took a while to take place. Hideki Tojo kept Bose waiting for at least three weeks and the two met only on 10 June. But once he met Subhas, Tojo was rather impressed and on 16 June, announced in the Diet—the Japanese Parliament: 'We are indignant that India is still under the ruthless suppression of Britain and are in full sympathy with her desperate struggle for independence. We are determined to extend every possible assistance to the cause of India's independence.'

Two days later the presence of Netaji in Japan was announced by Tokyo Radio with the Indian leader holding a press conference on 19 June detailing his plans for the freedom of his country. He called for the Quit India movement back at home to be escalated to an armed struggle. 'Only when the Indian people have received the baptism by fire on a large scale would they be qualified to achieve freedom,' he said. The news about Netaji's arrival in Japan electrified the Indians in Singapore and other South-east Asian countries. Soon Netaji was addressing them on radio. On 27 June 1943 Bose arrived in Singapore from Tokyo to a rousing welcome. He was accompanied by Rashbehari Bose. Singapore was destined to be Netaji's base for a good part of the next two years.

A week later on 4 July, at a public meeting, Rashbehari Bose officially passed over the mantle of leadership of the Indian Independence League and the INA to Netaji Subhas Chandra Bose saying, 'I have brought you one of the most outstanding personalities of our Motherland. I resign from my office as president of the Indian Independence League in East Asia. From now on Subhas Chandra Bose is your leader in the fight for India's independence.'

Netaji now announced that he would set up a provisional government whose task would be to prepare the Indian people for an armed struggle that would be the culmination of earlier efforts. He said, 'We have a grim fight ahead of us. In this final march to freedom, you will have to face danger, thirst, privation, forced marches and death. Only when you pass this test will freedom be yours.' Netaji's exhortations charged the environment and raised the morale of Indian nationalists in Southeast Asia. The Provisional Government of Free India was formally named as Arzi Hukumat-e-Azad Hind. The official language of this government was chosen to be Hindustani. To give legitimacy to the struggle for freedom, the Azad Hind government also developed its own civil code and released its own stamps. A bank was also formed a few months later in Rangoon.

On 5 July 1943 Netaji renamed the INA as Azad Hind Fauj and reviewed a march-past by the troops. Standing alongside Netaji was Prime Minister Tojo, who was on hand with material and moral support. In his address to INA soldiers Netaji said that every country that had won freedom had a liberation army leading the way. This included the United States under George Washington and Italy under Guiseppe Garibaldi. Netaji added, 'My soldiers, let your battle cry be "Delhi Chalo".' Bose also chose an anthem for the Provisional Government of Free India—Rabindra Nath Tagore's 'Jana Gana Mana'. Since the song was composed in highly Sanskritized Bangla it was translated into Hindustani. Netaji understood the importance of music in inspiring a force into battle and the translated anthem titled 'Subh Sukh Chain' was set to martial music. The other great song 'Vande Mataram', which had inspired the Indian freedom movement, was consciously avoided as an anthem. Netaji was sensitive to the fact that 'Vande Mataram', originally a poem in the novel *Anandamath* written in 1882 by Bengali writer Bankim Chandra Chattopadhyay and first sung by Tagore at the

1896 session of the Indian National Congress, could offend Muslims since it was written in the context of Hindu uprisings against the Muslims.

With his appointment as the head of the provisional government and INA, Netaji went all out to make his mission a success. At the end of July he began a tour of East Asian and South-east Asian countries to enlist the moral and financial support of resident Indian communities. Netaji got a rousing reception wherever he went: from Rangoon to Bangkok to Penang and Saigon. The expatriate Indian communities wanted freedom from the yoke of the exploitative British as much as the people back home. Fired by the oratory of Netaji and convinced of his earnestness and belief in the mission that he propagated, these Indians vied with each other to donate to the cause of freedom. There was nobody who did not contribute—businessmen, merchants, traders and workers—Bose is believed to have secured more than $2 million. Faced with the herculean task of raising and maintaining an army, Netaji had to go back to the people over and over again for money. In this effort he received support from unusual and unexpected quarters. For instance, in Rangoon a year later in 1944, when he urgently needed money he was pleasantly surprised when a local Gujarati Muslim Memon businessman Abdul Habeeb Yusuf Marfani donated his entire fortune of Rs 1 crore for the cause of India's freedom.

Armed with this money, Bose began mobilizing forces for the INA—his immediate target was 50,000 soldiers. Most of them would be enlisted from the POW of the British Indian Army and supplemented by civilian volunteers. In a revolutionary step for an army for Indians or any Asian country at that time, Netaji set up a regiment for women. This was appropriately named as the Rani of Jhansi regiment after the revolutionary leader of the 1857 War of Independence. Lakshmi Swaminathan, a successful gynaecologist from Singapore who was imbued with a revolutionary spirit was enlisted as the chief of the regiment.

It was a difficult task procuring weapons and ammunition for the fledgling national army and Netaji banked on the Japanese for assistance. Though willing to help the Japanese were fighting their own battles and were constrained by resources. The Japanese said that they could provide arms for only 30,000 soldiers.

Not to be deterred, Netaji went about setting up the provisional government that had to be operational before the Azad Hind Fauj went out to battle. The provisional government was officially announced on 21 October 1943 with Netaji as the head of the government and the supreme commander of the INA. It had five ministers: this included Anand Mohan Sahay who had migrated to the Far East in 1923 as a student and would become an activist with the Indian Independence League. On a trip back to India in 1927 Sahay had married the niece of the Indian nationalist Deshbandhu Chittaranjan Das and is said to have met Netaji who had just been released from prison in Mandalay. Sahay was put in charge of foreign affairs because he had been a resident of the region for a long time. He was officially not designated as the foreign minister, the portfolio was formally held by Subhas Bose himself. Subbier Appadurai Ayer, a correspondent for Reuters in Kuala Lumpur was appointed the minister for publicity and propaganda. One of the first declarations of the provisional government, which was taken a day after its promulgation, was to declare war against Great Britain and the USA. Some cabinet ministers were circumspect about declaring war on the United States but Netaji was insistent. Within days the provisional government began to be recognised by Axis countries and their supporters. This included Japan, Burma, Germany, Croatia, Italy, the Philippines and Thailand.

A few days later Netaji went to Tokyo to attend the Conference of East Asian countries. Since India was not part of East Asia, Netaji was invited as an observer, but allowed to deliver a speech. As usual in an impressive exposition he stressed the need for building a new Asia sans colonialism and imperialism. Even before the conference Netaji had requested Prime Minister Tojo to place the Andaman & Nicobar Islands that had been captured by the Japanese in 1942 under the administrative jurisdiction of the Azad Hind government. At the conference Tojo announced the decision of Japan to hand over the administration of the two islands to Azad Hind government. The handover took place in December 1943 and Lieutenant Colonel A.D. Loganathan was appointed chief commissioner. Netaji renamed the islands as Swaraj and Shaheed. It is said that the administration was nominally in the name of Indians and the Japanese rule continued. There are also reports of widespread violence by the Japanese on the civilian population of the islands. Netaji visited the islands just once but seemed to have been unaware of the Japanese high-handedness. The Japanese kept him away from the affected sections of the population.

Soon Netaji focussed his efforts on an attack on the Indian mainland through its north-eastern flank. With this in view he shifted the headquarters of the Azad Hind government to Rangoon in January 1944. Burma had earlier fallen to the Japanese. The first division of the INA was also shifted to Rangoon the same month. Lieutenant General Renya Mutaguchi, the chief of the Japanese Burma Area Army was responsible for the offensive through the north-east and very enthusiastic about the operation.

The Japanese and the INA had agreed that an attack into India should begin with Imphal in Manipur. This would mean a trudge through the Arakan mountains that led to Chittagong. While the British would use their resources to defend the Arakans to prevent Japanese entry into Eastern Bengal, other sections of the Japanese army with the INA would be able to penetrate and reach Kohima in Nagaland and Imphal in Manipur. This had to be achieved before the monsoons of 1944. With the advent of the monsoons, the rivers and rivulets would be flooded making transportation difficult. This would mean that the British Indian Army would not be able to rush in reinforcements from the rest of India. During a lull in the monsoons, the Japanese would break into Assam and Bengal.

Called 'Operation U-Go', the campaign was launched on 7 January 1944 but started rolling effectively only in the beginning of March.

Before that Subhas had personally supervised the battle readiness of the INA infantry division that would be part of the campaign, constantly exhorting them to the nationalist cause through inspiring speeches. As per the plan, one unit of the INA—the Subhas Brigade or the 1st Guerrilla Regiment was sent to the Arakan. This was to cover the left flank of the 33rd Division of the Imperial Japanese Army as it advanced. The 2nd Guerrilla Regiment of the INA was attached to the Japanese army's 15th Division. The Special Services Group re-designated as the Bahadur Group acted as scouts and pathfinders to the advancing Japanese units. They were also given the job of infiltrating British lines and encourage units of the British Indian Army to defect.

The combined campaign of the Japanese and INA took the British by complete surprise and they captured Kohima early on 6 April. Before that the Bahadur Group of the INA led by Colonel Shaukat Malik had broken through the British defences and set foot on Indian soil at Moirang in Manipur on 22 March. Netaji announced, 'We have now reached Moirang, the ancient citadel of Manipur. Our commitment is to march to Delhi and unfurl the Tricolour there. The expulsion of the enemy from the sacred soil of India is a compulsion for us. Freedom of India is very near.' Netaji was jubilant and in response to a call by him, Japanese Prime Minister Tojo announced that the conquered Indian territories would be put under the charge of the Azad Hind government. Immediately Netaji announced that his minister for finance Lieutenant Colonel A.C. Chatterjee would be the governor of these newly captured territories.

But soon the tide began to turn against the Japanese and the INA. There are many reasons for this including the fact that the Japanese had no airpower backing them. On the contrary the British used the Royal Air Force to bomb enemy lines. Since the Japanese (along with the INA) had to cross difficult terrain and routes over the mountains and jungles, they did not bring in field artillery, the chief anti-tank weapon, in large numbers. This was also under the mistaken belief that the British Indian Army would not be able to use their tanks on the steep jungle covered hills around Imphal (which is located in a valley). But in the event, the tanks were used to devastating effect. The British Indian Army also benefitted from sorties run by transport aircraft that parachuted supplies to them. In contrast the Japanese and INA supply lines were stretched. The Japanese had placed their reliance on Chenghis Khan rations—the Great Mongol in his numerous campaign used to drive cattle along with his army and these used to be the source of food. The Japanese had driven cattle from Upper Burma but most of them died due to lack of forage on the way. The Japanese could also not rely on the enemy for rations by taking away what the British Indian Army had.

Airpower stopped the advance of the Japanese and INA troops and allowed the British time to move troops to Imphal. British airpower was used to disrupt Japanese supply lines. This caused severe problems for the Japanese and the INA. Very soon for the Japanese and INA armies the offensive turned out to be defensive. After three months of siege in Imphal and at Kohima—some 150 km away from Imphal—the Japanese and the INA had to beat retreat. This was in the first week of July 1944.

The retreat was disastrous as the monsoons had begun. The soldiers had to trudge through the wet jungles and the roads were cut off due to the rains. In fact it rained so much that in some cases ammunition was swept off. Food was not available and disease broke out—from dysentery, cholera and malaria to beriberi and jungle sores. Many soldiers died of starvation and disease. Most of them were left unburied on the hills. The exact number of casualties have not been computed but conservatively was not less than 40,000 dead for the Japanese and INA together.

Netaji who was at Rangoon was stunned to hear of the retreat of the Japanese and the INA. Due to poor communication not all information was reaching him properly and in time. But true to his optimistic nature he announced, 'increase in casualties, cessation of supplies and famine is not reason enough to stop marching. This is the spirit of our revolutionary army.'

The defeat of the INA and the Japanese at Manipur was one of the turning points of World War II. British historians say that the Allied win in battle of Imphal and Dimapur was one of the biggest in World War II and ensured that the Japanese could not raise their heads again. Analysts also believe that if the INA and Japanese had launched the attack a year or two earlier they would have been successful. In the first phase of World War II, the British were on the backfoot and attack into India from the eastern sector could have jeopardized them. Unfortunately Netaji was in Germany that time and there was no INA. As far as the Japanese were concerned they did not want to launch an attack into India right after taking over Singapore in the fear that they would be seen as an army of occupation. By the time Netaji landed in South-east Asia it had probably become too late. Lastly the most important point to be noted is that the British fended off the INA and the Japanese with the help of the Punjab Regiments and the Gurkhas along with Scottish soldiers. In other words they used Indians to beat the revolutionary army of the INA. But this had been an old English device. In fact they held the Indian Empire serving British interests only with the help of Indian soldiers and even the soldiers of the First War of Independence in 1857 were defeated by the British with the help of Indian troops. The Imphal disaster—news of which trickled slowly—acted as a dampener to the Indian population in Malaya who were keen that the INA emerge victorious. Their morale plummeted and many who had been supporters of the INA and the Azad Hind government began shifting their allegiance fearing reprisals from the British. Meanwhile the Royal Air Force began bombing Penang, Kuala Lumpur and Singapore in a move that demonstrated their ascendancy in the skies. Netaji was still reiterating that the Axis powers would ultimately win the War—these assertions continued till November 1944. His belief was not shaken till the British neared Rangoon (using Indian regiments like the Sikh and Gorkha). With their backbone broken, the Japanese were interested in withdrawing from Burma to consolidate forces to defend their homeland. Their air and artillery power had been greatly depleted. In reality the British too were in a double mind about whether to recapture Burma or only parts of the country, realizing that the terrain was not favourable. However the Americans were interested in opening a route to China through Burma and the British fell to the pressure.

In September 1944 realizing that a herculean effort would now be required, Netaji raised the issue of suicide squads. The occasion was the death anniversary of the Indian revolutionary Jatin Das who had passed away after fasting sixty-three days in Lahore jail. Netaji said, 'The Goddess of Liberty is not appeased. I shall tell you the secret of appeasing her. Today she demands not merely fighters or soldiers for the Fauj. Today she demands rebels—men and women—who will be prepared to join suicide squads for whom death is a certainty. Rebels who will be ready to drown the enemy in the streams of blood that shall flow from their own body.'

But Subhas Bose was a realist too. Apparently at a meeting of the INA top bosses in January 1945 in Rangoon the issue of new war materials arriving on the Burma front from the USA (that was superior to that of the Japanese) came up. Along with this the subject turned to the increased incidence of desertions from the INA ranks. Netaji said, 'Our army is a volunteer organization. We have joined it not for the lure of money or rewards, but for sacrifice for the cause of Motherland. If anyone from amongst us be afraid of this poverty, hardship and death, he should not be sent to the front against his will.'

Bose continued to stay put in Rangoon and was not willing to leave the city. He felt that the city could be the staging post for another INA attack on India through Manipur once again. But this was not to be. As the British Army advanced into Burma and the Japanese began to leave, Bose was also forced to quit. But he did not quit with pleasure.

Netaji left Rangoon on 24 April 1945. While retreating—to Bangkok—Bose left a message for his faithful followers. 'Your brave deeds in the battle against the enemy on the plains of Imphal, the hills and jungle of Arakan and the oilfields will live in the struggle of Independence for all times. The future generation of Indians who will be born, not as slaves but as free men because of your colossal sacrifice will bless your name.'

Most of his men left by foot while Netaji was in a car. But after proceeding for some distance he realized that the ladies of the Rani of Jhansi regiment were also marching. They were not just on foot— they were marching bearing 20 kg loads. Upon learning this Netaji also started walking. On this march Netaji was solicitous about the safety of the injured, weak and sick and ensured that they were put on trucks though their numbers were limited and not everybody could be accommodated. Thus Netaji reached Bangkok only on 14 May 1945— on foot. From here he flew to Singapore, where he would stay put till mid-August, when he left for Saigon on what has been said to be his last journey. We know that this was not true.

10

Nehru, Mountbatten and Freedom

India's date with freedom on 15 August 1947 came about exactly two years after the Japanese announced their intention to surrender in World War II. It was not pure coincidence that India was granted freedom on this day. For Lord Louis Mountbatten, the last Viceroy of India, 15 August was a day of victory and celebration. In 1945 Mountbatten was the Supreme Allied Commander South-east Asia and was naturally overjoyed at the Japanese surrender.

But how was this linked to India's freedom? Surely India's Independence would not have been a matter of celebration for the British who were losing their 'jewel in the crown'. Herein lies a tale.

By the end of 1945, after World War II was won, the powers that be in Great Britain knew that the imperial game was over. Lord Archibald Percival Wavell, who was the commander-in-chief of the British Indian Army from July 1941 until June 1943, and subsequently the Viceroy of India till February 1947 remarked, 'our present position in India is analogous to that of a military force compelled to withdraw in the face of greatly superior numbers.'

Lord Mountbatten was sent to India with the express understanding that he would oversee the British withdrawal from India in such a way that would best serve the interests of His Majesty's government. This means that the successor Indian government would have to mirror—as far as possible—the British Indian government preceding it. There was logic behind this. Although the British were leaving India they were not abandoning their imperial possessions elsewhere. Primary among these was Malaya, their most profitable territory. The fiction of the British Empire had to be maintained and this could only be effective if India under the Indians was administered in a way similar to that of the British. More specifically the powers that be in London wanted a free India to be part of the British Commonwealth. This would in some way reinforce the fiction of the continuance of the British Empire.

The British had for long been sowing the seeds of communalism in the country. This was to culminate in the formation of Pakistan, with its western border perilously close to Afghanistan, through which it was feared the Soviets could descend. But having themselves promoted the Communal Award decreeing separate electorates for different religious groups in the country (introduced for the first time after the Minto–Morley report of 1909) there was nothing that the British could do now to turn back the communal clock. Contrary to public perception the first choice of the departing British was not a divided India exposed to Soviet influences through the North-west. There were signs that the Cold War was beginning and the British knew that Soviet expansionist dreams would have to be checked. Yet, when the communal ball that had been set rolling led to the demand for Pakistan, some sort of advantage was also seen in breaking up India (an entity that the British thought they had created). But that is a different story.

The onerous task of granting India independence and withdrawing from the country fell on the Labour Party government led by Clement Atlee that had won the elections in Great Britain at the end of World War II. The Labour Party had Fabian socialism among its core beliefs, a theory which committed to a socialist economy, alongside a commitment to British imperialism as a progressive and modernizing force. For the Labour government the Congress party with worthies such as Jawaharlal Nehru with his leftist leanings was closest to the philosophy of the party. It was also useful that the Congress leader was a product of the English public education system and therefore the British found it comfortable dealing with him.

The fact that Mountbatten and Nehru were personally close was an added factor. In fact more than Mountbatten, Nehru was closer to the Viceroy's wife Edwina, and by all accounts had an affair with her. This fact is not disputed. Veteran Indian diplomat and former foreign minister K. Natwar Singh wrote in *The Hindu* on 14 November 2008 that he had asked Vijayalakshmi Pandit of the purported affair. 'Of course,' she had confirmed. The only point of dispute was the nature of the relationship: was it sexual or was the affair purely platonic. But that is just a matter of detail.

In an interview to Indian journalist Karan Thapar in July 2007 in the programme *Devils' Advocate* on the CNN–IBN television channel, Lady Pamela Hicks, the younger daughter of the Mountbattens admitted that her father did use his wife's influence with Nehru on tricky matters of state. Lady Hicks said, 'My father, just in dry conversation, mightn't have been able to get his viewpoint over. But with my mother translating it for Panditji, appealing to his heart more than his mind ... that he should really behave like this. I think probably that did happen.' Thus Edwina became a bridge between the two men. In this particular instance, Lady Hicks was talking in the context of whether the issue of Kashmir should be referred to the UN. According to Hicks, the relationship was platonic. She writes as much in her book *India Remembered: A Personal Account of the Mountbattens During the Transfer of Power* and reiterated this in the interview with Thapar.

Over a period of time, the three became so close that when the Mountbattens left India, Nehru broke protocol and did the unthinkable. Natwar Singh reveals in his article in *The Hindu* that in a letter dated 21 May 1948 Nehru wrote to King George VI of Great Britain in terms unbecoming of a prime minister of a sovereign country, 'Shri Jawaharlal Nehru presents his humble duty to His Majesty. Lord Mountbatten made an outstanding contribution to the early and peaceful realisation of Indian Independence; as her first Governor-General, his advice and aid to his Ministers have been equally notable for their wisdom, sympathy and understanding. ... it is earnestly suggested that His Majesty be graciously pleased to confer upon the retiring Governor-General and his lady, some mark of recognition commensurate with these services.' (Mountbatten served for ten months as India's first Governor-General, right up to June 1948.) Not satisfied with merely writing such a letter, Nehru followed it up with the King's private secretary through V.K. Krishna Menon, the first Indian High Commissioner to the United Kingdom. On 29 July 1948, the King's private secretary wrote back to Nehru, in what can only be construed as a snub, 'His Majesty is of the opinion that adequate recognition has already been given (to Lord Mountbatten) and any further recognition would not be justified.' It is said that Nehru was so smitten with Edwina Mountbatten that he used to write to her almost every day and to ensure fast delivery Air India, India's national airline would ferry the letters across to the UK and bring back the reply on the return journey.

The point of relating all this is that Lord Mountbatten, who was not only aware of his wife's relationship with Nehru but also found it acceptable, used this proximity to influence the Partition of India and the future of Subhas Chandra Bose (as would best serve the British interests). The concept of Pakistan—a new homeland for the Muslims of India—was first propounded in 1933 and the Muslim League adopted a resolution in favour of the new country in 1940.

Nehru first met Lord Mountbatten and Edwina in 1946 in Singapore. India was poised for Independence and Nehru was treated as a hero by the expatriate Indian community. They were heartened by his presence in their city, more so because he had—not too long ago—donned his lawyer's robes and defended the accused in the INA trials at the Red Fort. At that time, Nehru, possibly to build a constituency amongst the Indian community proposed to visit Burma and Singapore. The British governor who controlled the Burma area refused permission. Mountbatten however saw an advantage in allowing Nehru to visit as a representative of the Congress party. He realized that freedom for India was around the corner and it made sense for him to cultivate a top leader of the party. Obviously Mountbatten saw a role for himself in India and had begun the spadework. Mountbatten ensured a hero's welcome to Nehru and travelled with him in an open jeep with the crowds cheering lustily.

The overjoyed Indian community requested Nehru to place a wreath at the INA memorial, erected on the seafront—at the insistence of Netaji during his last days in Singapore—by an Anglo-Indian officer of the INA, Colonel Cyril John Stracey. On reoccupying the city Mountbatten had ordered that the memorial be razed to the ground. Nonetheless thousands of Indians used to throng the site every day and place flowers in remembrance of the departed warriors. Nehru was to visit the site to place a wreath the day after the parade but never did. Why?

Amritlal Sheth, the eminent Gujarati nationalist and editor of *Janmabhoomi* newspaper was visiting Singapore around the same time as Nehru. On his return he reported to Sarat Chandra Bose that Mountbatten had informed Nehru that Netaji had not died in the so-called air crash and that he had authentic information to that effect. He had also told Nehru—in veiled language—that if Nehru demanded the absorption of INA men into the Indian Army, he ran the risk of presenting India on a platter to Bose when he reappeared. It is probable that this played on the mind of the ambitious Nehru, a political leader who had climbed the ranks of the Congress party on the coat-tails of Mahatma Gandhi. At a public meeting that Nehru addressed at Singapore's Jalan Besar Stadium before a crowd of 100,000, slogans of 'Blood, Blood, Blood,' were raised. This was the old INA chant but Nehru asked the crowds to refrain from mouthing such words and asked them to concentrate on constructive action.

Mountbatten's inner desire was to shoot Netaji on sight. In fact these were the orders of the British government at the insistence of war-time Prime Minister Winston Churchill. The instruction had been issued to the British Special Operations Executive (SOE) as far back as March 1941 and was never withdrawn. A 13,000 strong covert group, the SOE was set up to execute special tasks like subversion of the enemy, espionage, sabotage, special reconnaissance and assassination of select targets. Nicknamed the 'Baker Street Irregulars', the SOE was headquartered in London and had offices in Delhi and Cairo. The Delhi office was later shifted to Ceylon (Sri Lanka) and a mission came up in Singapore. The SOE decoded some intelligence in early 1941 (on the basis of an Italian telegram that it had intercepted) that Subhas Chandra Bose was travelling from Afghanistan to Germany via Iran, Iraq and Turkey. On receipt of this intelligence Churchill ordered that Bose be assassinated. The plan was to finish him off in Istanbul but as it happened, Bose took a different route to reach Germany and the SOE could not carry out the order. After Bose reached Berlin and the British came to know of it, the SOE personnel in Istanbul asked if the orders to assassinate Bose still stood. The British foreign office confirmed that it did.

Mahatma Gandhi was the tallest figure in the Congress but by 1946 he had ceased to be the most important person in the party. Nehru and Sardar Vallabhbhai Patel had marginalised the Mahatma and his views had very little relevance. Soon Nehru was to overshadow even Patel and in league with Mountbatten determine the destiny of millions of denizens of the country as it became free.

In February 1947, the Atlee government announced that India would be granted Independence by June 1948 and appointed Lord Mountbatten as the Viceroy. Mountbatten, an ambitious member of the extended British royal family owed his allegiance to Churchill, but quickly changed sides and swore loyalty to Atlee. This annoyed Churchill so much that after 1948 he refused to speak to Mountbatten. After arriving in India Mountbatten began to work closely with Nehru with whom he had been cultivating good relations since the Singapore visit. This suited both well. Mountbatten had control over the Congress through Nehru who in turn used his proximity to the last Viceroy to firmly establish himself as the most important person in the Congress party.

On 3 June 1947, Lord Mountbatten convened a press conference and announced some momentous decisions. Firstly India would become free by 15 August 1947. Secondly Sikhs, Hindus and Muslims in the Punjab and Bengal legislative assemblies would meet and vote for a possible partition of the country. If a simple majority of either group wanted partition, these provinces would be divided. The province of Sindh would take its own decision. The fates of the North-West Frontier Province and Sylhet district of Assam would be decided by referendum. Mountbatten also announced that a boundary commission would be established to determine the line dividing India and Pakistan in the event of the assemblies voting for Partition.

Mountbatten made this announcement fully aware that the Congress party would back the decision to partition India. Mahatma Gandhi had said a number of times, 'If the Congress wishes to accept Partition it will be over my dead body. Nor will I if I can allow Congress to accept it.' In the event he baulked and acquiesced. On the day that the announcement was made, Gandhi went on a *maun vrat* (literally, a vow of silence). The Congress party itself approved the proposal to partition India—a few days later—on 15 July after a vote was taken in the All India Congress Committee. The resolution was passed 157:29. The Congress Working Committee had already cleared the Partition plan— the very day it was aired by Mountbatten. Jawaharlal Nehru accepted the Mountbatten plan and broadcast, 'For generations we have dreamt and struggled for a free and independent united India. The proposals to allow certain parts to secede, if they so will, is painful for anyone of us to contemplate. Nevertheless, I am convinced that our present decision is the right one even from the larger viewpoint.' Armed with the stamp of approval from the Congress party, the British Parliament in July passed the Indian Independence Act. It was cleared without any objections or counters.

On the question of Partition the most interesting view came from Bengal where the assembly voted 126:90 in favour of unity of the province. When representatives of the Hindus and Muslims voted separately the latter were found to be against division and the former for it. In reality the majority opinion was for the province to be united but outside the Union of India. In public debates this view was championed by the most important Muslim League leader Huseyn Shaheed Suhrawardy and Sarat Chandra Bose. However Mountbatten in his 3 June proposal clarified that there could not be an independent Bengal outside the Union of India. So the idea of an independent Bengal did not get through leaving many in the province disappointed.

Mountbatten went about the partition of India—that would affect the life of some 350 million Indians—in the most cavalier fashion. He did not have any regard for the people whose fate lay in his hands. It was almost as if the Partition was rushed through to keep a date with 15 August. In early July, Cyril Radcliffe, a British jurist was flown into India and given just five weeks to demarcate the borders of India and the new nation of Pakistan. Radcliffe had never been to India before and had little clue about the country. He was provided rough maps made during the time of Lord Wavell. Two border commissions were set up—one for Punjab and one for Bengal with Radcliffe chairman of both. The commissions had four Indian members—two Hindus and two Muslims. In the charged environment just before Partition it was Radcliffe who had to take the call. All the members of the commission including Radcliffe were jurists and had little clue how to mark maps like a cartographer. There was very little time to obtain expert advice and as a result Radcliffe did a shoddy job demarcating 450,000 square kilometres of territory that sealed the fate of 88 million people. With a thick pencil the border was marked with little concern about geographical realities and where communities lived.

Radcliffe marked his maps and went back to Great Britain. The borders of India and Pakistan were only officially declared on 17 August 1947 two days after Independence. On the day of Independence people in Punjab and Bengal did not know whether they were in India or Pakistan. For instance, in Malda and Murshidabad in Bengal that had a majority of Muslims, flags of Pakistan went up on 15 August but two days later it was found that they were part of India. Similarly Khulna—in eastern Bengal—with a slight majority of Hindus was expected to be part of India but went to Pakistan.

The Partition brought mayhem in its wake and an estimated 200,000 to 500,000 people were killed in the violence that accompanied the process. An estimated 14 million people were displaced from their homes and most lost all their possessions as they trudged hundreds of miles across the border. It was a catastrophe of unprecedented dimensions that left a trail of death and destruction.

Could the Partition have been avoided? The answer is an unequivocal yes. The British were in a hurry to leave India. First, after having witnessed the popularity of the INA set up by Netaji Subhas Chandra Bose, the British could not have depended on the loyalty of Indian troops to defend India for them. After six years of war their strained soldiers were not ready to protect India. In these circumstances the Congress party should have held on—after all, freedom was round the corner. There was no way that freedom would be denied. The journalist Jayanta Roy Chowdhury, in his eponymous blog, writes a graphic account of how the popularity of the INA was threatening the British even after the War had concluded. He relates a memorable anecdote of Colonel Prem Kumar Sahgal (who married Lakshmi Swaminathan and was tried at the INA trial at Red Fort) when he was arrested and being taken in a truck to jail in Burma. Sahgal was being escorted by two British non-commissioned officers, a Punjabi Muslim Naik (equivalent to corporal) and four sepoys of the Frontier Force Regiment. On the truck the Naik told Sahgal that if he so ordered the British NCOs could be shot down and they could all get away. Sahgal knowing that the war was over asked the Naik to do nothing of that sort. In the jail the Colonel was accosted by twenty soldiers of the Madras Regiment who came to see him and said that their services and that of the entire regiment was at his command. In a parallel development Gurkha soldiers guarding Shah Nawaz Khan (who also stood trial at the Red Fort) sought discharge from their commanding officer to 'join the INA'.

Roy Chowdhury also points out how an anxious Sir Henry Joseph Twynam, governor of the Central Provinces wrote to the Viceroy, Lord Wavell on 10 November 1945 saying, 'When the airborne division leaves Bilaspore, I shall be left without British troops', while referring to frequent mutinies by Indian troops. Twynam also pointed out that in Jubbulpore (Jabalpur), when a speaker at a meeting asked which of those present would join the INA, all raised their hands.

On 24 November 1945 Field Marshal Sir Claude John Eyre Auchinleck, the commander of the British Indian Army, warned the British government of a full scale rebellion. He wrote: 'There are now large quantities of unlicensed arms throughout India and there will be many ex-INA men to use them.' He added that there were also a considerable number of demobilised soldiers (of the British Indian Army) who could do the same. The Field Marshal pointed out that the principal danger areas were likely to be the United Provinces, Bihar and Bengal but trouble must also be expected in the Punjab, Central Provinces and Bombay.

Jayanta Roy Chowdhury quotes Lieutenant General Srinivas Kumar Sinha (who after retirement from the Indian Army served as governor of the states of Assam and Jammu and Kashmir) who as a young Captain had been posted in the Army headquarters in the late 1940s. Apparently Sinha had managed to look into a note marked 'Top Secret—Not for Indian Eyes' prepared by the director of military intelligence Major General John Terence Nicholls O'Brien. In this report the emergency commissioned officers who were the largest body of commissioned officers in the British Indian Army numbering 12,000, were rated as 'highly suspect'. Regular Indian commissioned officers in the army numbering 400 were also labelled as 'not to be fully trusted.'

This note was sent to Auchinleck who in a report to the British Cabinet averred that 'most Indian officers are nationalists' and if the situation deteriorated they could not be relied on to defend India for the British. Auchinleck then asked for more divisions of the army from the British government. Britain, after the war did not have the numbers to spare, and could not raise more troops. According to Sinha the British were so nervous that they even formulated an evacuation plan called 'Gondola' to ensure the timely evacuation of 43,000 Europeans in case of a full scale rebellion. Even maps had been marked with evacuation routes to port cities. Thus, to reiterate, the British left India because they apprehended that they could be driven out.

The Cabinet Mission to India of 16 May 1946, initiated by Atlee, had come up with a proposal that could have avoided partition of the country. The Mission proposed that an Indian federation be created based on three groups of provinces. They were free to secede from the groups that they were placed in by a vote in the first general elections after the scheme took effect. However they could not secede from the Union of India. Thus, by this scheme, the unity of India would have been maintained. The government at the Union level would only deal with defence, foreign affairs and communications. The remaining subjects would be dealt with by the governments for each of the groups. However, they were permitted to confer other subjects upon the Union if they so wished.

Group A constituted territories that are all within present-day India—United Provinces, Central Provinces, Bombay, Madras, Bihar & Orissa. Group B consisted of Punjab, Sindh, Baluchistan and the North-West Frontier Province that are in present-day Pakistan. Group C comprised of Assam and Bengal.

Both the Muslim League and Congress were opposed to the proposals. Whereas the Muslim League supremo Mohammed Ali Jinnah was ready to consider the proposal when pressed, the Congress party wrecked it by categorically rejecting it. The proposal essentially involved the Muslim League and the Congress working together towards a structure akin to a confederation. The Congress however rejected the plan by saying that the states should have the right to secede from the group they were placed in immediately—if they so desired. Congress was also circumspect about allowing Assam to be clubbed with Bengal.

Whatever the consequences of the proposal, if this plan had been accepted, India would have gained freedom without division and the subsequent dislocation and loss of life would have been prevented.

In such a situation it is a moot question why Nehru and Patel were so eager to compromise with the British by agreeing to Independence at the cost of Partition. The commonly accepted logic is that they feared that they themselves could be pushed out from their dominant position by more representative public opinion. The two men were also advancing in age—Nehru was fifty-seven and Patel was seventy-two—and were in a hurry to reap the fruits of their labour. Nehru was quoted in an interview that he gave many years later to a British author as saying, 'The truth is that we were tired men and we were getting on in years too. Few of us could stand the prospect of going to prison again. If we had stood out for a United India, as we wished it, prison obviously waited us. The Partition was a way out and we took it.' This is a deliberate attempt to mislead because the British were in no position to imprison Nehru or anybody else after the War.

Nehru compromised and became the first prime minister of India. Mountbatten won his spurs with his masters back home since he had steered Britain through a tricky patch. But Subhas Chandra Bose remained locked up in a Soviet prison as all this happened. His presence would have changed the entire situation. It is easy to figure out that he would not have agreed to the Partition and would have strived earnestly to make common cause between the Hindus and Muslims. He would actually have waited for an appropriate opportunity to 'kick' the British out—literally.

11

Divided Bengal

The Great Calcutta Killings of August 1946, in which Hindus and Muslims butchered each other for over four days in the capital city of Bengal, is cited by historians as one of the main reasons that turned Indian sentiment towards accepting Partition. Since Bengal was the home province of Subhas Chandra Bose it is instructive to look at the politics and developments in the state about a year after his disappearance from public gaze.

The riots were set off by a call for Direct Action Day on 16 August 1946 by Mohammed Ali Jinnah after the failure of the Cabinet Mission Plan that year, which proposed a loose confederation for post-Independence India. The Muslim League headed by Jinnah demanded the creation of Pakistan. The League was then in power in Bengal, in fact the only province where they were running the ministry. Huseyn Shaheed Suhrawardy, the chief of the Muslim League in Bengal and also the chief minister of the province was committed to make Direct Action Day a great success in Calcutta (Kolkata). He had inexplicably declared a three-day holiday from 13 August. The exact sequence of events is unclear; however we do know that a major communal conflagration broke out in Calcutta on the appointed day and continued till 19 August. Some 5,000–10,000 people were killed in the riots and another 15,000 were injured. The riots were marked by intense brutality and bestiality.

The British police commissioner of Calcutta stood inert and his forces watched as the communal cauldron boiled over. He seems to have taken a detached view. As far as he was concerned the British were on their way out at the prodding of both Hindus and Muslims and he saw no reason to take active steps to control what according to him were their internal conflicts. The army had also not been deployed adequately and in time. The British governor of Bengal Sir Fredrick Burrows had answered this charge by asserting that he had deployed the army as soon as enough numbers could be mustered. It was only on 19 August that 45,000 British troops were deployed but by then much of the mayhem had already taken place.

Suhrawardy too did not cover himself with glory. In the midst of the riots he and some of his men were said to have stationed themselves in the police control room raising suspicions that they might have been trying to influence police operations. However Cabinet papers of 1938–46 now brought into the public domain show that Suhrawardy claimed that he went to the police control room to see how the police were working. At a 100,000 Muslim League rally at the Calcutta Maidan he apparently told his supporters that he had ensured that the police would be 'restrained' in taking action. The speech—in Urdu—is supposed to have incited the city crowds, a large section of which spoke the language as opposed to those from the countryside. Suhrawardy himself spoke Urdu and knew only a smattering of Bengali though this did not affect his wide popularity among the Muslims in the province. Among the Hindus, he never had a following, and was especially hated by the Marwari community who controlled trade and commerce. They alleged that Suhrawardy was communal and had connections with the underworld in the city. There was huge suspicion that he had played a role in exacerbating the effects of the Bengal famine of 1943 that had left a staggering 3 million dead. Suhrawardy is said to have patronised the black marketing of scarce grains by criminal elements and profiteering traders.

In Bengal of that era Muslims comprised 54 per cent of the population, Hindus 42 per cent, while the rest were Buddhists and other minorities. But in Calcutta, the economic powerhouse of the state, the population ratio was contrary to that of the province—there were 73 per cent Hindus while Muslims comprised 23 per cent. The remaining were Christians, Sikhs and other minorities.

The city of Calcutta with its port facilities and industrial establishments such as the jute mills held the key to the economy of Bengal. The second most important city in Bengal, Dacca (Dhaka, the capital of Bangladesh) was a pale shadow of Calcutta and a mere provincial town. While the jute mills were in Calcutta, the raw jute was raised in the fields of eastern Bengal. Thus it was imperative for anybody who wanted to reign over Bengal to control Calcutta. The Great Calcutta Killings are now essentially seen as an effort to gain control over the city and its resources.

The seeds of this conflict had been sown by the British as far back as the initial years of the twentieth century when a plan was mooted to divide Bengal. Huge protests had been triggered when the Viceroy, Lord Curzon bifurcated Bengal in 1905. Although Curzon said that it was a purely administrative decision since it was becoming difficult to govern the huge province, there were not many takers for this argument. The creation of two states would make administration easier, Curzon had asserted, pointing out that Bengal sprawled across 189,000 square miles and had a population of 7.85 crore.

Bengalis, specifically the Hindus among them, who were special beneficiaries of British rule in India and had empowered themselves through education, government jobs and business opportunities, were upset. They perceived this as a move to divide the Bengalis who had become stridently opposed to British rule in India. The division, they perceived, was an effort to reduce the clout of Bengalis and divide them on the basis of religion. This was not a wrong assumption because the new province, East Bengal—that was to be combined with Assam—would be a Muslim majority province. On the other hand, the remaining portion—Bengal would be a Hindu majority province. Yet Bengalis would lose their dominance in this province since it would also incorporate Orissa and Bihar. Whereas East Bengal would have 12 million Hindus and 18 million Muslims, the other part would have a population of 17 million Bengali speakers and 37 million Hindi or Oriya speakers. Thus Hindu Bengalis would lose their dominance across the new states.

Massive protests everywhere, which included the boycott of foreign goods put the government on the wrong foot. The leading lights of Bengal supported the movement—incensed as they were by efforts to divide the Bengali community. On 16 October 1905, the day the partition became operative, was observed as a 'day of mourning' with hundreds of public meetings. Speakers at these protest meetings declared that this was a classic case of the divide and rule policy of the British. The Bengali poet Rabindra Nath Tagore wrote *Banglar Mati Banglar Jol* (Bengal's Soil Bengal's Water), which became a rallying point for protesters seeking annulment of the partition. The movement lit up because of the support of the Hindu middle classes who used to dominate opinion in Bengal. The Congress party also supported the protests, further consolidating opinion against the partition, not only in Bengal but across India. The protests against the partition of Bengal soon took an anti-British colour. For the first time the opposition which had been, by and large, restricted to making petitions took the shape of a mass movement. Such was the fury sparked by partition that the British government had to reconsider its move. The government's administrative difficulties—the reason for the bifurcation in the first place—were not eased. Instead a spate of violence was let loose across Bengal with a revolutionary terrorist movement taking root. The British went all out to repress the protests and ordered a ban on singing the popular revolutionary song 'Vande Mataram' which was proving to have an incendiary effect on protesters. The subjugation of students and the press only increased the opposition. But what ultimately forced the British to reverse the partition was the boycott of English-made goods in Bengal. This included clothes and other commodities that were imported from England. Bengalis began to use locally-made—possibly inferior products. There was no second thought. The people's consciousness had been raised to a pitch and such was the anger against the partition that they persisted with their patronage of domestic products giving the English a lesson in the credo of indigenous self-sufficiency—*swadeshi*. By 1908 English commercial interests had begun to take serious note of their diminishing business returns created by the *swadeshi* movement.

The division of Bengal largely had support—in Muslim majority East Bengal. The opinion amongst Muslims was that through this bifurcation, East Bengal that had been a mere hinterland of the western half could now develop. Industries could come up and educational institutions could be set up. As if to support the move, the Muslim League was formed in December 1906 at Dacca (Dhaka). Around 3,000 delegates attended. The Nawab of Dacca, Salimullah Khan hosted the conference at his palace Ahsan Manzil and was one of the prime movers behind the formation of the party, though most of the delegates were from northern India where an unified Muslim consciousness was growing. The initiation of the League was a signal that East Bengal would also be a major centre for Muslim consciousness and identity.

In 1909, the government, in a move to control the adverse effects of the partition of Bengal and as a concession to the growing political consciousness in the country brought in what is called the Minto-Morley reforms. This allowed more Indian presence in the legislative councils both at the federal level and in the provinces. An Indian member was also inducted in the Viceroy's Executive Council. However for the first time, a separate Muslim electorate was created— by allowing Muslims to vote and elect Muslim councillors. This sowed the seeds of separatism and played a major role in affecting the politics of Bengal which we have seen earlier in this narrative.

Finally, in 1911, the partition of Bengal was annulled but at the same time the capital of India was shifted from Calcutta to Delhi. This was to undercut the importance of Bengalis.

The bloody Calcutta riots were followed by the Noakhali genocide two months later in October 1946. Whosoever may have been responsible for starting the Calcutta killings, rumours had reached Noakhali, a largely rural area in the Chittagong division in eastern Bengal, that Muslims had been targeted in Calcutta. Slowly anti-Hindu sentiments started building up in Noakhali with poets and balladeers whipping up the sentiments further. On 10 October 1946, on the auspicious first full moon night after Vijaya Dashami, when Kojagori Lakshmi Puja was being observed, a reign of terror was unleashed on the Hindus starting with the local *zamindar*. The violence continued over the next few weeks and affected an area of some 2,000 square miles (5,180 square kilometres). In an orgy of organized violence, thousands of Hindus were killed and hundreds of women raped in the villages. Many people were forcibly converted to Islam and many Hindu women married off to Muslims. Properties were systematically destroyed. There are no estimates of the deaths but it was only the Hindus who were killed. In the worst incident, a local *zamindar* (landowner) Rajendra Lal Chowdhury was attacked in broad daylight and his entire family of twenty-three was killed along with him. The incidents were planned to create terror amongst the Hindus systematically and ensure that they fled their homes. Nearly 1.5 lakh people lost their possessions, as the police were largely ineffective. The British government instead of trying to control the violence gagged the press. As a result the outside world received versions of what had happened from informal sources with the possibility that they were exaggerated and incorrect too. Of course, the riots were possible because the Hindus were outnumbered 4:10 by Muslims in the area. If the population had been balanced the chances of riots occuring would have been less. On 7 November 1946, shocked by what he had heard, Mahatma Gandhi reached Noakhali to restore peace and sanity. He stayed there for nearly four months till 2 March 1947.

The riots convinced the leaders of the Congress and the leading lights of Bengali society such as Syama Prasad Mookerjee that bifurcation of the province was the only way out under the circumstances. In this context it could be asked, if Subhas Bose had been present, how would he have reacted to the Calcutta riots and the Noakhali genocide? It is a no-brainer that the presence of a towering personality like Netaji would have gone a long way in cooling frayed tempers in Calcutta. Even a populist leader like Suhrawardy would have had to take cognizance of Netaji's views. Both Bose and Suhrawardy had started their politics swearing allegiance to the same man: Deshbandhu Chittaranjan Das. When Das became the Mayor of Calcutta in 1924, Suhrawardy was elected as the Deputy Mayor and Subhas Bose the Chief Executive Officer of the Calcutta Municipal Corporation.

On 27 April 1947, by which time the situation in Bengal had begun to be marked by distrust following the Great Calcutta Killings and the Noakhali incidents, Suhrawardy announced a new plan at a press conference in Delhi: of an united independent Bengal—separate from both India and Pakistan. Two days later, on 29 April, the same idea was announced in Calcutta by another Muslim leader Abul Hashim. A few days later, Sarat Chandra Bose, called for a Sovereign Socialist Republic of Bengal. He was supported by some other Hindu Bengali leaders like Kiron Shankar Roy (who became West Bengal's home minister after Independence). This was in part a reiteration of an earlier plan proposed by Sarat Bose in January 1947 for a socialist Bengal with its own constitution in the federal union.

On 20 May 1947 Bengali leaders formally announced a proposal for a united and independent Bengal. The proposal ran afoul of not only the Congress but the Muslim League as well. Sarat Bose also developed differences with Suhrawardy. Whereas Bose wanted a common electorate for voting and electing legislators, the latter insisted on separate electorates. This would have implied the same communal voting patterns that had been initiated in 1909. The Congress was wary that Suhrawardy's plan could be nothing but a covert attempt to hive off Bengal from India. But some Bengali Congress leaders had supported it because they saw Bengali unity (and thus a united Bengal) as a cause worth upholding.

It seems that Jinnah also gave his blessings to Suhrawardy agreeing to the proposition that Bengal without Calcutta meant nothing. He also hoped that independent Bengal would have good relations with Pakistan. But Jinnah's close followers like Maulana Akram Khan and Sir Khwaja Nazimuddin were opposed to the idea.

Suhrawardy thought a little differently; he knew that with a Muslim majority, he could control Bengal along with Calcutta if this plan was executed. Sarat Bose gave his assent to the plan because he was getting increasingly disenchanted with the Congress which he averred was taken in by Hindu interests. Moreover as a resident of Bengal he understood fully well that the economy of the province would be completely ruined if it was divided. He felt that Bengal would progress only if the province remained intact. The apprehension may not have been off the mark because West Bengal's fall from grace in the pantheon of Indian states began with Independence.

On 3 June 1947, barely fifteen days after the plan for an united Bengal was given concrete shape, Lord Mountbatten announced that India would be declared independent on 15 August 1947. The concept of an independent United Bengal was rejected.

The first partition of Bengal in 1905 was marked by heavy protests by the Hindu's even as the Muslims largely supported it. But the second partition in 1947 was due to fears from the Hindus that they would be swamped by Muslims and lose their identity.

But the million dollar question is whether Subhas Bose would have been inclined to accept an independent Bengal as proposed by his elder brother? It seems unlikely that he would have agreed. Subhas Bose was too big a leader to restrict himself to Bengal. A sovereign socialist independent India was the vision of Netaji—not a sovereign socialist independent Bengal. Thus the concept of a free Bengal would in all likelihood not have appealed to him. However, Sarat Bose's original idea of a socialist Bengal with its own constitution in federal India may have been agreed to by his younger brother, if a sovereign socialist independent India was not possible under any circumstances.

All said and done, Subhas Bose had the political skill to prevent a division of Bengal, as can be garnered from his ideas expressed during earlier elections in the province. When Bengal went to polls in March 1946, the Muslim League virtually made it a referendum on partition. On this basis the League got 115 of the 250 seats in the assembly but fell far short of winning a majority. So the majority was still not in favour of partition. The Congress got eighty-seven seats and the Europeans (who had a separate electorate) picked up twenty-five. Apparently Suhrawardy was not even sure of the loyalty of some of his League members like Akram and Nazimuddin who he believed would forsake him on the floor of the assembly. So Suhrawardy started talking to the Congress on the back-channel through Kiron Shankar Roy about some sort of alliance in forming the government. On his part, Roy took the matter to Congress president Maulana Abul Kalam Azad. The latter belonged to Calcutta and approved the alliance with the understanding that the Muslim League would only have one more minister than that of the Congress. However the plan could not be implemented because Suhrawardy insisted that the Congress could not nominate any Muslims to join his ministry. There was also a demand that the home minister should be from the Congress. In the end, Suhrawardy formed a ministry with the support of the Europeans. It was an all-Muslim cabinet with not a single Hindu minister. Aware of this criticism, Suhrawardy inducted Jogendra Nath Mandal, the Bengal chief of the All-India Scheduled Castes Forum as a minister. This set the tone for increased tensions between the Hindus and Muslims who began to feel that Suhrawardy's actions had a hostile intent.

As late as 1938, the Congress party could have taken steps to stem the rise of the Muslim League and prevent the partition of Bengal. Subhas Bose had at that time proposed a Congress-Krishak Praja Party (KPP) tie-up but his idea was shot down by Gandhi. The KPP though a largely Muslim supported party represented the interests of the peasantry and thus was not communal.

It so happened that in the Indian provincial elections in 1937 the Congress party had won the maximum number of seats in Bengal even though they could not garner a full majority. But the policy of the Congress was to form governments only where it held a majority. Thus Sarat Bose, when invited to form the government, was unable to take up the offer. Subhas had not participated in the elections. The party which came second—KPP—then sought to form the government. The party was led by Abul Kasem Fazlul Huq who was basically a leader of peasants. The KPP's manifesto included scrapping the Permanent Settlement of 1793—in effect the abolition of *zamindari*—and free universal education. With his first choice for a coalition partner, the Congress party being ruled out, Huq then formed a government in collaboration with the Muslim League. The League represented the interests of north Indian landlords and the feudal classes of the United Provinces. Thus there was an inherent contradiction between the interests of the KPP and the League. Moreover the League had grown on communal lines unlike the KPP which represented the interests of the small farmers. This was the reason why it was popular.

One man who realized this inherent contradiction was Subhas Bose. In 1938 he returned to active politics and became the president of the Congress. Bose approached Mahatma Gandhi and told him that there was a case for toppling the government and forming a Congress-KPP alliance for which Huq would be game. Gandhi gave the impression that he agreed but later changed his position. He wrote to Bose from Wardha in December 1938 that after an 'exhaustive discussion' with Maulana Abul Kalam Azad and the industrialists Ganshayam Das Birla and Nalini Ranjan Sarkar he had come to the conclusion that the Congress would in no way gain by ousting the Bengal ministry. An incensed Subhas wrote back to Gandhi a few days later: 'The letter came as a profound shock to me. I remember to have discussed the Bengal situation with you time and again. The other day at Wardha it was discussed between us once again. The papers say that after I left Wardha Sjt. N.R. Sarkar, Sjt. G.D. Birla and Maulana Azad Sahib have seen you. Evidently, you have altered your view after talking to them. The position, therefore, is that you attach more value and importance to the views of those three gentlemen than to the views of those who are responsible for running the Congress organization in Bengal.' Sarkar, an industrialist from Bengal, was an acolyte of Birla and had joined the Huq ministry as finance minister in 1937.

It was a historic blunder on part of the Congress not to go into a coalition with the KPP since the Muslim League made full use of the opportunity afforded to them. Soon Fazlul Huq got caught in the vortex of the League's politics. Jinnah realized that Huq was an invaluable asset and weaned him into the Muslim League and made him move the Lahore resolution (now called Pakistan resolution) in 1940 asking for a homeland for Indian's Muslims—Pakistan. Before that even the Muslim League had not dreamt that they could get Bengal into their programme for Pakistan. The Muslim League got stronger in Bengal and there was no let-up in the spate of communal riots.

Huq, a leader of peasants, soon realized that the League was making full use of him and decided to break out of the party. He started negotiations with Sarat Bose, Syama Prasad Mookerjee and some scheduled caste leaders to form a progressive coalition. Getting wind of all this, the core League ministers in the Huq government resigned in December 1941 to put pressure on him. But within days, Huq resigned and formed a fresh ministry with Syama Prasad Mookerjee as his finance minister, and two ministers from the Forward Bloc—the political formation that had been set up by Subhas Bose in 1939 after he resigned from the presidency of the Congress. Bose himself was in Germany by this time. This government was seen as pro-public even as Huq and Mookerjee toured districts calling for communal amity and asking Muslims to defend temples and Hindus to defend mosques.

But soon the external situation began to change. The Quit India movement was kicked off by the Congress and later as the World War intensified the Japanese threat increased. The popular government had become powerless with the bureaucracy under the Governor assuming all powers. The Quit India movement was especially strong in districts of

Bengal like Midnapore, where the police came down on protestors with a heavy hand. In the name of controlling law and order they resorted to cruelties and even raped women. So insensitive had the British become that when Fazlul Huq promised to order an inquiry on the high handedness of the police, the British governor asked him in writing to refrain from making such assurances. Meanwhile the League under Suhrawardy also saw an opportunity and began to heckle and criticize Huq saying that he had become a renegade and collaborated with the Hindus. In popular perception, Huq's popularity went down due to circumstances outside his control. With the Japanese threat looming large (the Japanese had begun air raids on Calcutta and other parts of Bengal), the Muslim League began to poison the ears of the Governor that the provincial government should be dismissed because it had two ministers from the Forward Bloc whose leader Bose was a renegade who had joined the Axis powers. Finding that he was powerless, Syama Prasad Mookerjee also resigned. In his resignation letter he pointed out the chicanery of the British who were depending more on official advice than that of the elected government established after elections. Syama Prasad also accused the Bengal governor, John Arthur Herbert of holding a brief for the Muslim League. A few months later—in July 1943—Herbert outmanoeuvred Huq and had him ousted. Needless to add, a League government was established even as a man-made famine engulfed Bengal. It is believed that Herbert had a go ahead from the bosses in Delhi for his machinations. With Subhas Bose having landed in Singapore the British were worried about him and averred that he would take Japanese help to attack Bengal. In these circumstances they did not want an independent premier like Fazlul Huq in Bengal. They wanted a pliant Muslim League man and they found one in Khawaja Nazimuddin. What marked the tenure of Nazimuddin's government—which did have a few Hindu ministers—was the great Bengal famine which was man-made. Described as Churchill's secret war, food grains were procured in huge quantities for allied soldiers and exported elsewhere, leaving little for the local population. In the meantime, apprehending a Japanese attack, all boats and various other means of navigation that could be used to transport grains were destroyed. At the same time large tracts of land were kept fallow—with the possible aim of depriving Japanese invading armies from accessing food grains. The famine was an unprecedented calamity for Bengal and as said earlier in the chapter resulted in millions of deaths. The English Raj in Bengal that started in 1757 was followed by a famine in 1770 that resulted in the wiping off of one third of its population. Now the Raj was coming to a close with a huge famine and loss of life.

12

The Mystery of Gumnami Baba

In the late 1970s and early 1980s there were rumours that a holy man had taken refuge in Faizabad town in the state of Uttar Pradesh. That man in all probability was none other than Subhas Chandra Bose. Although the rumors were more or less locally confined, word somehow reached Bose's niece Lalita in Calcutta. The daughter of Suresh Chandra Bose, Lalita decided to travel to Faizabad and investigate the matter herself. What she saw put her in a quandary. 'She got the impression that the holy man who went by the name of Bhagwanji could be her uncle. His mannerisms were the same and the handwriting matched exactly. But she had a little doubt. She said it's too close to take a call,' recalls her nephew Amit who lived in the United States in those days. Lalita is now dead. But it seems that the doubts arose because she was meeting her uncle after nearly forty years. In these long years age had caught up and the appearance of the holy man appeared haggard, although he had a spiritual aura around him. Bhagwanji himself was not ready to reveal his identity directly.

For the record Lalita had known Subhas Bose closely. The Suresh Bose branch of the Bose family lived in the same house as Subhas on Elgin Road in Calcutta and this had allowed Lalita to fraternize with her uncle—more than some of her other cousins who lived in different houses across the city.

In 1986, a few months after Bhagwanji passed away, Lalita moved the Lucknow bench of the Allahabad High Court with a writ petition to seek an official inquiry into the identity of the holy man. She was joined by Dr M.A. Haleem, vice-president of the All India Socialist Party and Viswabandhav Tiwari, the vice-president of the All India Subhas Mukti Vahini. The court gave its final verdict only in 2013 although it passed an interim order soon after the petition was filed. More of that will be discussed later in this chapter.

Going by whatever information is available, Bhagwanji who was also known as Gumnami Baba arrived in the ancient town of Ayodhya—Faizabad's twin city—in 1974. The circumstances under which he arrived there and from where are not known precisely. However it is believed that he came to Ayodhya from Basti, a district headquarters town some 70 km from Ayodhya on the Indo–Nepal border. There are multiple versions of his early days in Ayodhya. According to one version his first stop was the Gurudwara Brahmakund Saheb—located on the outskirts of Ayodhya—where he stayed for six months. The gurudwara—which is very old and had been visited by three Sikh gurus in their time—overlooks the river Saryu. Old timers recall that the Baba used to meditate at a spot in the gurudwara that had a view of the vast catchment area of the river. They also remember how he was quite disciplined about his meditation. The other version however is that on arrival in Ayodhya the Baba rented a part of a building in the Lakhnauti Mata area and stayed there for many years. This was a rundown dilapidated structure with no electricity and some of the people this author spoke with swore that they knew for sure that the Baba lived there. In those days however people referred to him as *pardey wale baba*—because he spoke from behind a *parda* (curtain)—a trait that was to define his interactions with outsiders.

The Baba seems to have been keen to avoid too much publicity. According to Rita Banerjee, a resident of Faizabad, Baba had told her father-in-law Dr T.C. Banerjee that he was a *sannyasi* (monk), forbidding the latter to talk about him. A popular homeopath in

Faizabad with an established practice, Dr Banerjee was one of the first persons in their household to have met Baba, and was also his personal physician. Rita Banerjee told this (and much more) to *The Times of India* correspondent Arunav Sinha in an interview in late June 2015. Baba seems to have had a hypnotizing effect on people—apparently he had an intense gaze—so intense that it was difficult to look straight into his eyes. He was also fond of typical Bengali delicacies like *shukto*, *ghanto* and *keema*. However Baba would only converse in Hindi even if members of the Banerjee family spoke to him in Bengali. Clearly, Baba wanted to keep his identity a secret. In November 1983 Gumnami Baba shifted into Ram Bhavan, a house on the now busy Faizabad–Ayodhya Road and a stone's throw away from the Circuit House in the Civil Lines area of Faizabad. He moved in along with his caregiver Saraswati Devi Shukla whom the Baba called Jagadamba. Saraswati Devi had been with him even during his stay at the Gurudwara Brahmakund. In fact it was because of Saraswati Devi that the Banerjee family had come in contact with the Baba. She had come looking for a doctor and had run into Dr Banerjee. The Banerjee family became close to the Baba and were the only ones who had free access to him. In fact, Rita disclosed to Arunav Sinha that Gumnami Baba used to address her affectionately as *phulwa rani* (flower queen) and her husband Priyabrata as *baccha* (child). After Dr Banerjee passed away in 1983, Priyabrata took over from his father as Baba's physician. In a video interview to *Mission Netaji*—a group of young Indians trying to uncover the mystery behind the disappearance—Priyabrata recollected the day his father went to meet Baba for the first time. He said that his father went in to meet the Baba sometime at 11 am or 12 noon but came out only around 4 pm and on returning exclaimed that he had just met Netaji Subhas Chandra Bose. The son asked, 'How do you know?' The father replied that he recognised Netaji because he had seen him earlier but that Baba had forbidden him to talk about the meeting.

So, how did Baba move into Ram Bhavan, his last home where he passed away three years later? Thakur Shakti Singh, the present owner of Ram Bhavan told Arunav Sinha that his father Gurubasant Singh a retired city magistrate had been approached by Dr Raghunath Prasad Mishra, a surgeon at the district hospital to rent out the rear portion of his house that had an independent access. Dr Mishra said that he was looking at the house for his *dada* (grandfather) who wanted to do spiritual exercises in a peaceful and tranquil environment but was unable to do so at home.

Shakti Singh said that Bhagwanji had a very strict policy regarding visitors. He would meet only a select few and that too late in the evening after he had finished his *sadhana* (spiritual practices). This would only be after 8 pm. The spiritual exercises could extend for long periods. In fact, the Baba used to perform his *sadhana* twice a day, once in the morning and once in the evening. Those who met Bhagwanji came back with the feeling that he had some special powers. Apparently those who entered Ram Bhavan felt that their mental faculties had been overwhelmed by Bhagwanji. The *sannyasi* kept himself veiled from his interlocutors with an ochre-coloured cotton curtain. Thus nobody got a chance to see Bhagwanji directly. Even Shakti Singh who stayed at the same house never got a chance to meet Bhagwanji face-to-face. Word soon got around about the mysterious *sannyasi* and a police officer known to Shakti Singh evinced a keen interest in probing the mystery of who the holy man really was. One morning the officer arrived with a few policemen but the moment he entered the compound of Ram Bhavan something seems to have happened and he abruptly turned back. He was probably overwhelmed by some unknown force. The same evening the Baba called Shakti Singh and asked him: 'Why did your friends not come in this morning and introduce themselves?' After that the Baba laughed loudly.

In normal circumstances the Baba spoke with a heavy voice and was crisp in his speech. Many who heard him wondered whether he had been a military general earlier on.

Giani Gurjeet Singh of Gurudwara Brahmakund Saheb, who had seen Bhagwanji when he had stayed at the gurudwara remembers the glow and radiance on the face of the holy man. 'The spiritual glow was blinding and cannot be described,' he told Arunav Sinha. In an interesting incident, the Giani recollects that while Bhagwanji was there he realized that the children staying in the gurudwara premises were deprived of milk. Immediately he called for the chief priest and paid out money instructing him to buy a buffalo. In the video interview with *Mission Netaji*, Priyabrata Banerjee also spoke of Baba's intense spirituality, which anyone in his presence could discern. Surajit Dasgupta of Kolkata who was introduced to the Baba by some of his disciples met him for the first time in 1982 and many times after that. He told *The Times of India* correspondents Saikat Roy and Shubro Niyogi that among other things Gumnami Baba predicted the disintegration of the Soviet Union and remarked that Communism will die in the place of its birth. Dasgupta who was also under instructions to never look at the face of Gumnami Baba once had the irresistible urge to steal a glance. What he saw was a replica of Netaji but with thinning hair and flowing beard. But the eyes were powerful and Dasgupta says that he realized that the Baba had reached a higher place of existence and had become a *mahatma* (a venerable person).

Gumnami Baba died on 16 September 1985. If indeed he was Subhas Chandra Bose—as it now seems likely—he was a grand old man of eighty-eight when he passed away. In the last year or two of his life he was plagued by severe arthritis that had left him bound to a wheelchair. The Baba was cremated in secrecy at night. His body was carried in a small bus to Guptar Ghat on the banks of the Saryu where legend has it that Lord Rama had walked on water. It was a small group of thirteen people who accompanied the Baba on his last journey. They included Saraswati Devi Shukla, Panda Ram Kishore (with whom the Baba had been in touch even before his arrival in Ayodhya), Priyabrata Bannerjee and the Baba's other followers, Virendra Rai, Gopal Krishna Srivastava and Dr Raghunath Prasad Mishra. Apparently an emotional Ram Kishore had exclaimed, 'We are only thirteen people here, there should have been 13 lakh people.' More people would have probably attended had the funeral not been organized in a hurry, and cloaked in secrecy. The body was not cremated at the regular burning ghat, but a little away from it. Another poignant fact: in Uttar Pradesh and across north India bodies are never cremated at night. However in Bengal bodies are cremated at night. So, was this funeral that of a Bengali gentleman, and was he Netaji?

As a mark of respect to the Baba a rock was placed to mark the spot where his body had been consigned to the flames. But a few years later the locals felt that a memorial at the spot was necessary to do justice to the memory of the Baba. Accordingly, a marble memorial now stands at the spot, which is now seeing an increasing number of visitors. It is also a fact that more people in the region began to hear of Gumnami Baba after his death than when he was alive.

Much after his death, stories began to circulate that Baba had been seen in many other places of Uttar Pradesh. One version has it that he had lived in Naimisharanya (Neemsar) in the Sitapur district near Lucknow before he moved to the Ayodhya-Faizabad area. This is an ancient Hindu religious site and is even mentioned in the Ramayana and considered an ideal location for undertaking spiritual exercises. This version says that before Naimisharanya, Baba had lived in Basti. Perhaps he had shifted to Basti once again before ultimately going to Ayodhya. He is supposed to have left Basti because the local populace had started speculating whether he was Netaji. Three witnesses testified before the Mukherjee Commission that they had met him in Basti. Apurba Chandra Ghosh who had known Subhas Bose from his Calcutta days testified that he had met the Baba in 1965 when he was living as a *sannyasi* in Basti and twice after that. Ghosh claimed that the Baba had asked him about Bahadur, the *durwan* (watchman) at the Bose residence on Elgin Road in Calcutta and wondered whether he was still there. He also inquired if there was a calendar with Goddess Kali's image in the guard-room. A second witness Durga Prasad Pandey testified that he used to meet the Baba regularly—almost every night—for a long period in 1967 in Basti. Another witness Shrikant

Sharma said that he had met the Baba in 1963 in Naimisharanya. Both Sharma and Pandey had seen Subhas Bose before he had disappeared from India in 1940. All these witnesses asserted that the Baba was indeed Netaji but could not provide any photographic evidence of their meeting that would have helped the Commission to come to a decisive conclusion. According to a story titled 'Netaji, The Saint?', published in *The Times of India* on 5 September 2015, a follower of Subhas Bose discovered Baba by pure chance. Atul Sen was visiting various places in Uttar Pradesh in 1962 when he heard of a Bengali *mahatma* living in an ancient Shiva temple in Neemsar. Curious, Sen went to the temple and it took just a few interactions for him to realize that this man was none other than Netaji.

It is also not clear when the locals in Ayodhya-Faizabad who had met Gumnami Baba first began to believe that he was actually Netaji in disguise. The first person who thought so was the elder Dr Banerjee and slowly the word spread through him—albeit in hushed tones. Not everyone thought that the Baba was Netaji but respected him nevertheless. According to newspaper reports, while testifying before the Mukherjee Commission Dr Raghunath Prasad Mishra said, 'I had never seen Bhagwanji from Netaji's point of view but he indeed was a great personality. He possessed deep wisdom and great powers. He had wrested from nature mastery over forces invisible and intangible.' However, many locals feel that Dr Mishra was not stating the entire truth, as we shall see below.

After the death of the Baba the legend of Netaji spread due to a variety of reasons. *Nai Log*, a newspaper published from Faizabad, speculated extensively on whether Gumnami Baba was in fact Netaji. Later two other English language dailies picked up the refrain—the *Northern India Patrika*, an English newspaper published out of various places in Uttar Pradesh as well as the *Amrita Bazar Patrika* published out of Calcutta. More importantly the possessions of the Baba that were found in Ram Bhawan showed that he was no regular monk. The collection included books such as Alexander Solzenitsyn's *Gulag*

Archipelago, Brigadier J.P. Dalvi's *Himalayan Blunder* (which provides an account of the Indian debacle at the hands of the Chinese in the 1962 war), the *Dissentient Report* by Suresh Chandra Bose and the dissenting view of Justice Radhabinod Pal in the trial of Japanese war criminals. Also found—the complete works of Shakespeare, many classics written by Charles Dickens including *A Tale of Two Cities*, Lewis Carroll's *Alice in Wonderland*, novels written by P.G. Wodehouse and the *Rubaiyat* of Omar Khayyam. Maulana Azad's seminal book *India Wins Freedom*, Sitaram Goel's *Nehru's Fatal Friendship* and many books on contemporary politics written by Kuldeep Nayar were also part of the collection. Long-playing records of K.L. Saigal, Nazrul-geeti (songs by Kazi Nazrul Islam), Bismillah Khan's *sehnai* and Ravi Shankar's *sitar* recitals were also found in the Baba's abode. This list is not exhaustive but there were German binoculars, a Corona typewriter, a Rolex wristwatch, maps and numerous newspaper cuttings including a series on how the Taihoku plane disaster was a concocted story.

The details of these possessions became public after the Lucknow bench of the Allahabad High Court asked for the preparation of an inventory of these items through a court commissioner, in its interim order on 10 February 1986. S.N. Singh, the president of the Bar Association of Faizabad, who was appointed as the commissioner was stunned to find a lot of objects relating to the INA, framed family photographs including that of Subhas Bose's parents and reports of committees set up to probe his disappearance. Incidentally the photograph of Bose's parents were adorned with flowers everyday by the Baba, confirming in a way that the latter was none other than the Indian leader, says journalist V.N. Arora, who along with a few others had represented to the district magistrate to break open the locks of the Baba's quarters that were sealed on his death. Arora told this writer that when he examined the room it became clear to him that all the belongings that one would expect to find in Netaji's room were there. Moreover, the man who had lived in that room had been a highly spiritual person and was certainly not an imposter.

Letters from Samar Guha, Leela Roy and Pabitra Mohan Roy were also found amongst the possessions of Gumnami Baba. Guha was a Member of Parliament from the Praja Socialist Party and had taken up the issue of the disappearance of Netaji many times in the Lok Sabha. In fact, he had even written a book on the subject. On 22 January 1979—with the Janata government in power at the Centre after the Emergency years—Guha released a picture that he claimed was that of Netaji taken a year back in a temple. He asserted that Netaji was living in intense *tapasya* (meditation) for the unfulfilled mission of his divine motherland. Guha said, 'My moral responsibilities impel me to let the people know that Netaji is alive.' He also said that Netaji was in jail in the Soviet Union for many years. Stories suggest that the Baba was very angry with Guha for making the revelations and refused to meet him after that. That Gumnami Baba was very particular about keeping his identity under wraps is no secret. Apparently he had made associates like Dr Raghunath Prasad Mishra take a pledge of secrecy. Journalist V.N. Arora reveals that he saw the original print of the photograph released to the press and published in *The Statesman* among the collection of objects from the Baba's room along with a copy of the newspaper clipping. Arora told this author, 'There were newspapers which were marked with Baba's comments.'

Samar Guha died in 1991. Leela Roy was a close associate of Subhas Bose and had moved to the Forward Bloc the moment it was founded. This was unlike many Congressmen who were otherwise loyal to Subhas Bose but preferred to stay on. Pabitra Mohan Roy was from the INA Secret service. He had been dispatched by Netaji on a Japanese submarine to India. His job was to set up a radio transmitter at Behala close to Calcutta to disseminate Subhas Bose's messages. He was caught in the act, put on trial and sentenced to death. The sentence was later commuted to life imprisonment.

According to Arora, the body of Gumnami Baba lay for two days before it was cremated. This was because Dr Mishra said that he was contacting Netaji's relatives and would wait for them to come. Mishra did not say which particular relative he was contacting or how. This led to bewilderment among others who knew the Baba. In the end Dr Mishra hurriedly organized the cremation without informing many, says Arora. After the cremation, Dr Mishra put his lock on the Baba's quarters, angering other followers. Two other followers then put their own locks on the quarters leading to confusion. By this time word was spreading that the Baba was none other than Subhas Bose in disguise, leading to considerable curiosity. It was then that many concerned citizens of Faizabad including Arora had the district administration break open the locks. 'We concerned citizens were allowed to get into the room for half an hour. But we came out after eight hours, so vast was the range of things in the Baba's rooms. It was an amazing exercise.'

The most serious effort to examine whether Gumnami Baba was Netaji was made by the Mukherjee Commission. The Commission ordered the matching of the Baba's handwriting—both in English and Bengali—with that of Netaji Subhas Chandra Bose. Unfortunately the reports that came up were contradictory. B. Lal, former Government Examiner of Questioned Documents confirmed that both the English and Bengali handwritings of Baba matched with Netaji's writing samples. But in a joint report, Amar Singh and M.L. Sharma from the office of the Government Examiner of Questioned Documents said that there was no match. This was also the opinion of Dr S.K. Mondal of the Forensic Science Laboratory of the Government of West Bengal.

Nine teeth that had been found in the quarters of the Baba in Ram Bhawan were also sent off by the Mukherjee Commission to the Central Forensic Science Laboratory in Kolkata for DNA profiles. This drew a blank. The expert Dr V.K. Kashyap reported that the teeth belonged to an old male. However, he said that the DNA of the teeth did not match with the DNA of blood samples taken from Netaji's relatives both from his father's side and his mother's side. On this basis, the Mukherjee Commission concluded that the Baba was not Netaji (though this was stated in an indirect way in the report). Strangely the teeth which were sent off for DNA examination were found in empty match boxes. Moreover the DNA test was undertaken some two decades after they were discovered. It is not impossible that the teeth were replaced by some interested party—who had knowledge of medical science—within days of the Baba's death.

In a strange twist of affairs, a video tape of an off-the-record conversation between Justice Manoj Kumar Mukherjee and a film producer captured the former saying that it was his belief that Gumnami Baba was in fact Netaji. In fact he had no doubt on this, the retired Supreme Court judge said. The producer Amlan Kusum Ghosh had been interviewing Justice Mukherjee for his documentary *Black Box of History* but after the interview had ended, the video had still been rolling and Justice Mukherjee made these comments without realizing this. In fact he said on tape, 'Please do not quote me on this.'

On 30 January 2013, nearly twenty-six years after the original petition had been filed by Lalita Bose and much after her own death, the Lucknow bench of the Allahabad High Court delivered the final judgment on the matter. The Court directed the Uttar Pradesh government to form a panel to probe the identity of Gumnami Baba alias Bhagwanji. The division bench of Justice Devi Prasad Singh and Justice Virendra Kumar Dixit said: 'The state government is directed to consider for appointment of a committee consisting of a team of experts and higher officers headed by a retired judge of the high court to hold an enquiry with regard to the identity of the late Gumnami Baba alias Bhagwanji. Let a decision be taken expeditiously, say within a period of three months.' The bench also directed the state government to consider establishing of a museum at Faizabad 'where the articles of the late Gumnami Baba may be kept under the supervision of a qualified person.'

Although two and a half years have elapsed between the issuance of the directive and the publication of this book, the Uttar Pradesh government has still not moved on the orders. There is no panel to

The Mystery of Gumnami Baba

enquire into the identity of Gumnami Baba as yet. In mid-July 2015 however, the state government announced that it would house items and personal belongings of Gumnami Baba at a Rama Katha Sangrahalaya. The government of Uttar Pradesh has provided Rs 1.5 crore in a supplementary budget for creating a separate section in the Sangarahalaya that would be dedicated to Gumnami Baba.

Gumnami Baba was not the first holy man to be declared as Netaji. In fact the stories about the Baba were only locally known in Faizabad and Ayodhya. But the legend of the sadhu of Shaulmari had spread far and wide. The story goes something like this: around 1959, a *sadhu* (monk) who was called Sharadanandji by his disciples set up an ashram at a place called Falakata in Cooch Behar district of West Bengal. At first nobody took notice of the ashram or the *sadhu*—till the area in which the ashram was located expanded dramatically to 100 acres. The number of residents in the ashram also went up—to about 1,000. What began to cause consternation were the armed guards posted at the gates of the ashram. At this point rumours started spreading that the *sadhu* was none other than Netaji Subhas Chandra Bose in disguise. Within a year or so—by 1961—rumours had spread like wildfire and this was remarkable considering that there was no television, internet or social media in those days.

To check the veracity of the rumours, Major Satya Gupta who had been an associate of Netaji in the Bengal Volunteer Corps in the late 1920s met the *sadhu* at the ashram in February 1962. He came back to Calcutta and called a press conference and declared that the *sadhu* was none other than Netaji. The reports of the press conference were published in the newspapers on 13 February 1962. After that many reputed people individually visited the ashram. Some declared that the *sadhu* was indeed Netaji while others declared that there was no likeness. Among the visitors was Pradeep Bose, son of Suresh Bose, who was convinced that the *sadhu* had nothing to do with Netaji. However Pradeep Bose, who is no longer alive, had told his relatives that he was impressed by the military-like precision and organization with which the ashram was run. This would remind anyone of Netaji since he was known for his great organizational skills. However the matter of the *sadhu* rose to a crescendo before dying out. In the interim it became a subject of parliamentary discussion as well.

The *sadhu* stayed in the ashram for nearly seven years and thereafter shifted to Dehra Dun where an ashram was set up on Rajpur Road for him. He died there in 1977 and was cremated in Haridwar. Notably some old associates of Netaji believed that he indeed was the man and went to the funeral. Among them was Uttam Chand Malhotra at whose house Subhas Bose had taken refuge in Kabul when escaping to Germany.

The issue of this *sadhu* being Netaji was also examined by the Mukherjee Commission. The Commission had also received contradictory reports from witnesses but concluded that the *sadhu* was not Netaji. The witnesses on whom the Commission relied on had stated that the *sadhu* had himself declared many times that he was not Netaji. The Commission noted that although the *sadhu* spoke Bengali it was in a dialect used in Sylhet district of undivided Bengal. On the other hand Subhas Bose's family hailed from West Bengal and he had grown up in Cuttack.

Although some of the witnesses before the Commission declared that the *sadhu* himself had discounted the possibility of his being Netaji, he had not made these claims loudly enough to be known publicly and allowed the rumours to persist. In fact, with the benefit of hindsight it seems that the *sadhu* was being directed by certain highly skilled people with a pre-determined strategy. This accounts for the sudden growth of the ashram and the military-like precision with which it was run. Though no conclusive proof can be produced it is not inconceivable that this was a Government of India operation run through the Intelligence Bureau or a similar organization. In those days Jawaharlal Nehru was the prime minister and was increasingly under attack for keeping the matter of Subhas Bose' disappearance under wraps and not making efforts to unravel the mystery. Since Netaji's spiritual inclinations was no secret, if a *sadhu* was set up as Netaji there would be many who would accept this story. This would take the focus away from the real Netaji—who the powers that be presumably knew had arrived in India quietly and was living in obscurity. Interestingly the focus on Shaulmari Baba diminished after 1966 when he went to Dehra Dun and lived in relative obscurity. Notably by this time, Nehru had passed away.

13

The Transformation

It was the middle of the night in the dead of winter in Ayodhya. The temperature was low—barely a degree or two above freezing point. Gumnami Baba was sleeping inside the room. Panda Ram Kishore was sleeping outside with an *angeethi* to stay warm. Suddenly he realized that the Baba might be cold too. He got up with a start and went inside and asked: 'Baba do you need the *angeethi*?'

Baba answered: 'This body has lived in Siberia. You keep the *angeethi*. I don't need it.'

Nobody knows when Subhas Chandra Bose transformed into Gumnami Baba and when he was released from the Siberian labour camps. Much of what is written in this chapter is interpretative and based on information which is incomplete in parts. Without interpretation and intelligent extrapolation it would not be possible to even guess what happened to Netaji once he gave up to the Soviet troops in Manchuria after the faked air crash.

It appears that Bose was imprisoned in two different labour camps in Siberia. In all possibility, Netaji was at first placed in the harsher labour camp in Yakutsk in Eastern Siberia.

In normal circumstances, Bose could have been expected to have perished in Yakutsk and lie interred under the infamous 'Road of Bones' built by conscripted labour. But he was probably shifted away from Yakutsk, to a gulag in the steppes of Central Asia, north of Mongolia where the climate was not as harsh. This internment camp was close to Lake Baikal, the deepest lake in the world which is now an UNESCO heritage site.

That Bose was in Yakutsk can be deduced from the testimony of former diplomat and parliamentarian Satya Narayan Sinha to the Khosla Commission—that former NKVD agent Kuzlov had seen Bose in Cell 45 of Yakutsk Prison. That he was interned in a gulag close to Lake Baikal was also revealed by Gumnami Baba in the course of his cryptic conversations with his disciples.

Why Bose was shifted can only be speculated upon. There is no firm evidence in the public domain till now. May be one day when the KGB archives and that of other Soviet agencies are opened, confirmed information will be available. But it is equally possible that nothing will be found because millions of prisoners were interned in the gulags. Whether Stalin's men kept detailed records for posterity is at best a matter of conjecture. But as analyst Anton Vereshchagin—writing in a different context—says in an article published on 10 October 2013 in the *Russia & India Report*: 'Joseph Stalin had relatively tense relations with Jawaharlal Nehru and could hardly miss an opportunity to influence him. Keeping Bose under his control could have been a nice trump card to use against India's first prime minister.'

Word may have reached Stalin or some of his close confidantes that Bose was unlikely to survive Yakutsk. But if he was useful as a trump card, as a threat to Nehru, then it would have to be ensured that Bose did not die in Yakutsk. So he had to be shifted. In another version Netaji was imprisoned in Omsk in south-western Siberia. The following anecdote might explain why he was shifted. Jyotiranand Maharaj, who has headed the Ramakrishna Mission in Moscow for the last two decades, revealed two years ago that his research indicated that after learning of Netaji's presence in a jail Vijayalaxmi Pandit had wanted to see the Indian leader. Although she was allowed to visit the jail, she was denied permission to go into the cell that housed

Netaji. However in the course of her visit, says Jyotiranand Maharaj, she came across a totally exhausted prisoner who looked startlingly like Netaji. The person seemed to have been physically tortured and was in a somewhat mentally unstable condition. It seems that Pandit rushed back to India within a week of her visit to Omsk, ostensibly for consultations, but nothing came out of it. The Maharaj did not reveal the source of his information. Perhaps there is some record in India's embassy in Moscow.

An assessment based on geopolitical realities would seem to suggest that Netaji was probably kept in an internal security jail or perhaps in a security home for about a year and a half or two years after his surrender and thereafter packed off to a labour camp. Considering that he surrendered to the Soviet security forces in the second fortnight of August 1945, Netaji must have been transferred to the gulag by August 1947. In other words, as India got its freedom, the man who waged a war for Independence was pushed deeper into the abyss.

In the first place, why Bose was transferred to a gulag, is in itself not clear. Did his actions offend Stalin? Was Stalin persuaded by British intelligence reports that Bose was a MI6 agent? In the totalitarian system fostered under the Soviet leader, even the simplest of things could have caused offence, with the 'punishment' often being disproportionate. Contemporary events in North Korea, where ministers have been put to death for disagreeing with the dictator, is a good example of the workings of a totalitarian state. In fact, even when Bose was in Germany, there was always a danger that he would be sent to a concentration camp. It is only because his friends in the Reich had kept him protected that Bose was safe. Perhaps in the Soviet Union, Netaji ran out of luck or could not find such friends to lobby for him at the Kremlin.

Though Netaji may not have had the opportunity to meet Stalin, he had probably convinced some other functionary of the Soviet Communist party to allow him to raise an army like the INA to raid India from the north-west through Afghanistan. This seems to be a likelihood considering the report of Major Hugh Toye of British intelligence. In a report in 1946 he said, 'The Governor of the Afghan province of Khost has been informed by the Russian ambassador in Kabul that there were many Congress refugees in Moscow and Bose was included in their number. There is little reason for such persons to bring Bose into fabricated stories. At the same time the view that Bose is in Moscow is supplied in a report received from Tehran. This states that Moradoff, the Russian Vice-Consul General, disclosed in March 1946 that Bose was in Russia where he was secretly organizing a group of Russians and Indians to work on the same lines as the INA for the freedom of India.' (This report has been quoted by Netaji researcher Purabi Roy in her article 'Tracing the Footprints of Bose' published in the *Pioneer* on 24 September 2005.)

If these reports are correct it would mean that Netaji's work in the Soviet Union would have come to a halt once Britain granted freedom to India on 15 August 1947. There was now no need to invade India to free it from foreign domination as had been envisaged by Netaji. Moreover, with the bifurcation of India, an invading force moving through Afghanistan would have to cross Pakistan. In any case Soviet support for Netaji in raising a national army for the liberation of India would never have been as whole-hearted as that of Japan. Though the beginnings of the Cold War were already discernible as World War II drew to a close it was doubtful that Stalin would openly support Netaji's wish to liberate India with Soviet help and thereby openly come into conflict with its ally Great Britain.

It was after India became independent and, as speculated in an earlier chapter, after the matter of Japanese war criminals had been dealt with that Netaji was sent off to the gulag. Significantly Purabi Roy who has done considerable research about the presence of Netaji in the Soviet Union wrote in the *Pioneer* that a Soviet agent called V.G. Sayadiants who lived in Mumbai and sold Soviet periodicals, literature and records was in touch with political leaders. According to Roy, Nehru handed over a letter to Sayadiants in August 1946, requesting that it be delivered personally to Stalin. The contents of the letter are not known. However it may be speculated that since India was soon expected to gain freedom (although the official announcement came a few months later in February 1947) Nehru must have sought Stalin's support for India. This implied that Stalin should support Nehru.

It can be safely concluded that Bose would not have been in Yakutsk beyond 1949 or 1950. Life in the camp near Lake Baikal was probably somewhat better than his earlier prison. This camp comprised petty criminals and a large number of political prisoners. Those who were labelled petty criminals were probably not wrongdoers by any stretch of imagination. Among them were employees who had reported late for work more than three times. Also included were common people who had been caught cracking jokes about government officials. As for the political prisoners, they were mostly citizens who had resisted the forced occupation of their countries by the regime led by Stalin—Ukrainians, Belarusians, Estonians, Lithuanians and Latvians. Most of them were kept under detention without trial or were imprisoned after summary trials on trumped up charges. There were poets, professors, artists, singers and other talented and educated persons in captivity who were made to do gruelling work while being exposed to the elements.

Many of the gulags did not have properly demarcated boundaries. So any prisoner could have escaped to freedom. It was still a difficult proposition and most never made their way out once interned. The gulags were located in the middle of nowhere. The harshness of the weather also dissuaded many prisoners from attempting to flee the gulags. There are instances of fleeing prisoners falling victim to snow blizzards and others losing their way. Besides, after some prisoners started fleeing, the gulag administrators brought in tracking dogs which could sniff out the escapees. Later a system of rewards was also instituted—people who lived around the gulags were rewarded if they caught and brought in an escapee.

At the beginning of 1953, 2.4 million prisoners were held in the gulags and of this 465,000 were political prisoners. They were held in

450 labour camps. Bose was probably one of them. After the death of Stalin the number of gulags was reduced and many prisoners were released. It was at first gradual. After Stalin was denounced during the Khrushchev regime, the release of prisoners accelerated. It would not be unreasonable to expect that Bose was also probably released in this process.

It is instructive to note that almost 500,000 Japanese soldiers and officers of the former Kwantung Army in Manchuria were arrested as prisoners of war (POW) by the Soviet forces in 1945 as the war ended. Although POWs, they were sent to labour camps and made to do rigorous work. An estimated 60,000 died in the camps. It is only around 1948 that the Japanese began to be released. This process continued for three years, till 1950. But all the Japanese were not released—for alleged crimes of war—and languished in the labour camps for decades. Since Bose surrendered to the Soviet Army in Manchuria, it is a moot point whether he was clubbed along with the Japanese and packed off to Siberia. We have no specific information on this.

In 1956, the book *The Long Walk* was unveiled to rave reviews and ultimately sold half a million copies. A movie was also made out of the memoir of Slawomir Rawicz, a Polish prisoner of war held in Irkutsk, a place in the coldest region of north-east Siberia. He recounts his escape from Camp 303 under the cover of a blizzard and the 6,000 km trudge to freedom. Accompanied by six more escapees, Rawicz walked ten months to reach India. The fugitive party included three Polish soldiers, a Polish girl, a Latvian landowner, a Lithuanian architect and an US metro engineer. The journey took the group through the Gobi Desert, China, Tibet and the Himalayas. On the way, four escapees died: two in the Gobi desert and two in the Himalayas. The remaining three reached India in an emaciated condition and were found by a Gurkha patrol in the Himalayas. The escape journey was undertaken in 1941. But later the memoir was challenged by some who pointed out that the journey never took place because Rawicz was released directly in Iran in 1942. Thus he could not have undertaken the journey. But there were others who pointed out that the journey was real and that somebody instead of Rawicz had undertaken the travel. A British intelligence officer in India—Rupert Mayne—also confirmed that three emaciated men had been debriefed by him in his office in Calcutta in 1942 and had pretty much told him the same story about the long march. However, when he was quizzed many years later, he could not remember the names.

Was it that Bose had a similar impulse when he was released? The distance between Lake Baikal and Gorakhpur is 3,608 km—which is just sixty per cent of the long walk undertaken by Rawicz and the other five escapees. The route would entail crossing Mongolia and China into India through the Himalayas. So if Netaji had trekked across this terrain he would have had to take the same route. We also do not know whether he came alone or had other compatriots. Another relevant point to ask—if Bose was let off officially, why had he not contacted the Indian authorities in Moscow from where he could have been repatriated home? There are no answers for this: the only possible explanation, he must have realized that he was not welcome among the ruling establishment in India. This is a realisation that must gave come early, even before he was despatched to the gulag. It is not unrealistic to assume that Netaji did make an attempt to communicate with Stalin and even contacts in India while he was being held in the internal security jail.

'If Gumnami Baba was indeed Subhas Bose it is clear that he did not enter India without coordinating with his network of associates and well-wishers. Entering India and settling is not possible without the help of other people,' says Amit Mitra, West Bengal's finance minister and the grand-nephew of Subhas Bose.

Cut to Faizabad in India's Uttar Pradesh. V.N. Arora, who had entered Gumnami Baba's quarters in the town after he passed away, remembers seeing a map that charted the route that the Baba had taken from Siberia to India. Presently the map is locked up in the Faizabad treasury. 'The map gave the coordinates of the area through which he passed and most of it was in China,' Arora remembers. But the map did not mention the mode of conveyance taken by Gumnami Baba—whether he travelled by road or by foot or by a combination of various modes. Arora adds, 'Gumnami Baba's room had a huge amount of handwritten notes. Nobody has read them till now. May be once these papers are made public we will get a clue about his journey and who knows, even his life story. For all we know he might have left his life story in writing, yet to be discovered he might have left his life story in writing that has not yet been discovered. Nandalal Chakravarti, a former professor of political science, who chanced on a copy of the map told the Kolkata edition of *The Times of India* recently that it mentions places and mountain regions visited and routes traversed by the Baba. Locations are indicated by surrounding cities, mountains and rivers. On the left is Afghanistan, at the top left is Tajikistan. The line stretches to Kashgar, Yarkhand in the middle at top and then on to Kiyuchen of China on the right. Also mentioned is Stalinabad, the name of Dushanbe between 1931–61. Dushanbe is the capital of Tajikistan and the fact that the name Stalinabad is mentioned would mean that the Baba had traversed the place before 1961, avers Chakravarti. Ashok Tandon, a journalist from Faizabad who had made a copy of the map from the belongings of Baba says that 'it is clear that the Baba had unusual acumen in geography.' Even before he was seen in Naimisharanya, Gumnami Baba reportedly first showed up around 1962 in Etawah in western Uttar Pradesh though the year is disputed. The city is on the Delhi–Kanpur railway line and there are stories that he was patronised by the Raja of Etawah. 'I would imagine that he showed up shortly after Nehru's death,' says Arora and bases his opinion on the fact that the Baba kept old newspapers stacked in his room. 'We found copies of the *Pioneer* with him dating back from late 1964,' he says.

Since Netaji had once run away from home for a year on a pilgrimage to holy places, it would not be unreasonable to expect that he would have tried to find refuge in spirituality on his journey back. In fact even while in Siberia he might have taken recourse to spirituality to overcome the incredibly difficult time that he was going through. 'This is not at all an unrealistic assumption,' says Mitra. It is possible that Bose may have punctuated his long journey back to India with spiritual exercises in the Himalayas. This would account for the fact that if he was released around 1959, he was seen in India only in late 1962 taking an incredibly long three years to journey. Probably these spiritual exercises in the Himalayas transformed Bose into Gumnami Baba. V.N. Arora recollects that while leafing through a copy of the book *Himalayan Blunder* by Brigadier J.P. Dalvi, found among the possessions of Gumnami Baba, he was startled by the notes on its margins. One of these clearly mentioned: 'You fool I was there. This is not what had happened.' Arora says he can't remember the exact reference and whom the Baba was labelling as a fool. The controversial book, banned immediately after it was published (later the ban was lifted), dealt with the Indo–China War of 1962 and the events preceding the conflict.

Incidentally the name Gumnami Baba translated into English will mean the 'lost saint' or the 'nameless saint'—in other words a man whose identity had been erased. This labelling has a connection with the prisoners of the gulags who felt that they had lost their identity. 'Zvat' NIKTO, familiya—NIKAK' is what the prisoners would say of themselves when being taken to the gulags. In English this translates as, 'My name is nothing. My family is nobody.' Was the name Gumnami— without a name—inspired by a stint at a gulag?

When the story of Gumnami Baba began to circulate many said that he could never be Netaji Subhas Chandra Bose. After all, the great Indian leader was a man of action. Bose could not have remained in virtual hiding. At least that is what Gumnami Baba's reticent lifestyle would seem to indicate, the spiritual practitioner who preferred to remain low-key.

Though this is no exact parallel, in India there is an example of a revolutionary turning into a spiritual leader. This is the case of Aurobindo Ghosh who transformed into Sri Aurobindo. Ghosh started his life in the Baroda Civil Service serving the Gaekwads of

Baroda after returning from England. He had qualified in the Indian Civil Service exam but since he did not pass the horse riding test he was not offered the job. Some argue that he deliberately failed the horse riding test by reaching late for the exam. After a few years in Baroda, Ghosh returned to Bengal where he was influenced by the revolutionary activities. Aurobindo was arraigned in the Alipore Bomb case in 1909 and kept under solitary confinement. He turned to spirituality in jail where he heard his inner voice. In the end he was acquitted. Later a warrant of arrest was again issued against him—this time for some of his writings. Aurobindo scooted to the French colony of Pondicherry and took refuge there. In Pondicherry Aurobindo metamorphosed into the spiritual guru Sri Aurobindo.

If Aurobindo could transform into a spiritual leader, there is no reason why Subhas Chandra Bose who had seen life more closely and intimately, could not have followed the same path. However Sri Aurobindo, who had a big ashram in Pondicherry had the Mother, his chief disciple to administer what became like an empire. The ashram continues even till today because of influx of followers who set up home there. But Gumnami Baba showed no tendency to organize any ashram or take in followers barring less than the half-a-dozen who looked after his needs and with whom he discussed subjects that interested him. Thus Gumnami Baba had remained largely unknown. This was also because he himself made an effort to keep away from public view.

Gumnami Baba, though endowed with spiritual powers retained a bit of his worldly desires. Little wonder then that cartons of 555 and bottles of Scotch whisky were found in his room after his demise by V.N. Arora. In a video interview with *Mission Netaji*, Rita Banerjee more or less confirmed that Baba had been a smoker. When asked whether Baba was a smoker, Rita said, 'shayad (probably)', but hastened to add, 'He never smoked before us.' As stated in an earlier chapter the Banerjee family knew the Baba closely and had access to him. A non-vegetarian, tobacco smoking Baba may have raised the hackles in many parts of India but not among followers of the *Shaivaite* cult or those who worship *Shakti*. This reservation would be limited to followers of the *Vaishnavite* cult which stresses on vegetarianism.

In some respects Gumnami Baba demonstrated contradictory tendencies. He stayed for some time in a dilapidated run-down building in Ayodhya that did not even have an electricity connection. At the same time he used to partake of only organic vegetables and grains specifically grown for him by Panda Ram Kishore. This was revealed by V.N. Arora who added, 'The living standard of Baba was high and if he ate *poori* it had to be fried in pure *ghee* and what is more the left-over *ghee* could not be used for refrying; it had to be mandatorily thrown away. Otherwise the Baba was a small eater.' Panda Ram Kishore was a wealthy priest, one of the few *tirth purohits* in Ayodhya. *Tirth purohits* are found at Hindu religious places and maintain records of families for generations. Thus they are a source of family histories. Panda Ram Kishore revered Gumnami Baba and in turn the latter also thought highly of him and addressed him as Nand Baba.

Surprised by the strenuous efforts made by Gumnami Baba to keep away from the public eye, those who had access to him would ask him the reason. The Baba would say that the time was not yet ripe to reveal himself. Yet, on a few stray occasions he is also said to have indicated that he was none other than Bose. He had once asked the members of the Banerjee family to look at him carefully: '*Dekho dekho, main Subhas Bose toh nahin?*' (Have a good look, am I not Subhas Bose?)

14

Was Netaji Forsaken by His Own Government?

As soon as it became clear that the air crash in which Netaji was believed to have died could have been faked, the Government of India started making frenetic efforts to figure out where he was and what he was up to. Simultaneously, senior government officials launched a strenuous campaign to convince the public-at-large that Bose had perished in the air crash at Taihoku on 18 August 1945.

Common people and even many at high places were taken in by this steady messaging, but the Government of India—by this time India had won freedom—knew that the information that they were putting out for public consumption was incorrect. Thus it is clear that the government initiative to look for Netaji had not been planned with any altruistic motives: it was designed to checkmate the patriot.

At the beginning even the government was not sure of the leader's whereabouts. Therefore, it began spying on Bose's close relatives in the hope that crucial information about the activities of the leader would come out of this snooping. It was believed that Netaji would get in touch with his relatives either directly or indirectly. In fact the snooping continued till 1968—some twenty-one years after Independence—demonstrating the high degree of interest shown by the government to ferret out the truth about Bose.

That the government was trying to mislead the public had always been suspected but now, with the benefit of hindsight, we also know that the central government's Intelligence Bureau (IB) worked hand in glove with the MI5, the national security intelligence wing of the British government, in this activity. This knowledge has become public with the declassification of official records in the United Kingdom. The intelligence cooperation began as India became independent, a time when the new regime in India was expected to strike an independent line. A story published in the 12 April 2015 edition of *The Times of India* with the revealing title—'Documents Reveal Nehru Government Shared Information on Netaji with MI5' reported that not only did the Nehru government snoop on Bose through the IB but also shared confidential information with the MI5. On 6 October 1947, IB official S. Balakrishna Shetty sought the comments of the MI5 on a letter that it had intercepted. The letter was written to Amiya Nath Bose, a nephew of Netaji's by A.C.N. Nambiar who had been the leader's deputy in Germany. Nambiar stayed in Zurich. Shetty said in his request letter to the MI5's representative in Delhi, K.M. Bourne that the Nambiar letter 'had been seen during secret censorship and passed on. We shall be grateful for your comments.' In turn Bourne forwarded the letter to his director-general in London with the comments: 'Any comments that you make in this letter will be appreciated. The letter could be about Bose's wife and daughter though the context is unclear.'

In the same edition of *The Times of India*, a former RAW special secretary V. Balachandran was quoted as saying, 'IB had played a junior partner to MI5 even after 1947 and this was similar to what it was before Independence.' He went on to point out that this collaboration continued all the way till 1975. After the transfer of power, the MI5 positioned a Security Liaison Officer (SLO) in New Delhi as its representative. According to the declassified archives the deal was done by Guy Liddel, deputy director of MI5.

Over a period of time, the dependence of the IB on MI5 increased and strangely enough the IB started following Britain's intelligence priorities. Bhola Nath Mullick, who served as the organization's chief from 1948–68, is known as India's intelligence czar. But now it seems that he was a czar only in name. The declassified British archives suggest that he 'encouraged' Walter Bill, then SLO, to visit the IB's headquarters to see its work on 'preventing communist subversion.' In 1957 he wrote to Roger Holly, MI5 chief, 'I never felt that I was dealing with an organization which was not my own.'

When moves to rescind links with the MI5 first cropped up in 1971, IB director S.P. Verma was devastated. He wrote to the MI5 chief, 'how would he manage without a British SLO.'

Balachandran pointed out in *The Times of India* story that Christopher Andrew, the official MI5 historian concludes, 'Nehru either did not discover how close the relationship was, or less probably did discover and took no action.' Balachandran warns that 'this needs to be kept in mind before concluding that Nehru ordered IB snooping on Netaji's family'.

This is letting Nehru off the hook. In all probability, the Nehru government was trying to run with the hare and hunt with the hound. On one hand it wanted to use the IB to keep a watch on the Communists—in effect, on the Soviet Union where Netaji was supposedly located—while on the other hand, the regime was trying to foster a closer relationship with that country. Christopher Andrew, in an interview to *DNA* newspaper on 2 May 2010 revealed that the IB had contacted MI5 for a specialist to analyse data that it had collected on subsidies given by Moscow to the Communist Party in India. Incidentally Anuj Dhar, who is engaged in unravelling the Netaji mystery, says that Bhola Nath Mullick, as IB chief had lied to the Khosla Commission and misrepresented to the Shah Nawaz Committee. Dhar said in an interview to the *Zee News* television channel on 10 August 2012 that Mullick had doctored the Japanese version of a British-era report on Netaji's purported death by removing the final passages before presenting it to the Shah Nawaz Committee. He also alleged that if statements under oath made by Mullick to the

Khosla Commission is compared to facts now emanating as a result of a Right to Information (RTI) query filed by him, then the former IB boss would be found to have committed perjury. Mullick died in 1984.

The IB collaboration with British intelligence ceased only after Prime Minister Indira Gandhi told the IB czars to discontinue it. Balachandran, in *The Times of India* story says that he was present at the meeting where Indira Gandhi spoke to IB bosses. After 1970 and more specifically after the Indo-Pakistan war in 1971, India became closer to the Soviet Union, with whom the country had signed a friendship treaty. Since the IB–MI5 deal was basically to keep tabs on Communist countries, the closer ties with the Soviet Union led to excising of ties with British intelligence agencies.

Not only was the IB snooping on Netaji's relatives but Nehru personally also sought to find out about their activities. As a result of another RTI query, we now know that Nehru wrote a letter on 25 November 1957 to the then foreign secretary, Subimal Dutt about Amiya Nath Bose's visit to Japan. Nehru wrote, 'I would like to find out what he (Amiya Bose) did in Tokyo? Did he go to our embassy? Did he visit the Renkoji temple?' Amiya Nath Bose, the eldest son of Sarat Chandra Bose, became a Lok Sabha MP in 1967; but in 1957 he had been a mere barrister. So there was no reason for Nehru to enquire after Amiya Nath's activities in Japan unless of course he was paranoid that Netaji was alive and would surface some time.

Chitra Bose, daughter of Sarat Bose, told *The Times of India* in April 2015 that she recollected a visit by Nehru to their residence in Calcutta shortly after the air crash. 'Panditji showed father a rectangular wrist watch with a charred band and said with teary eyes—this was the watch Subhas was wearing when the crash took place.' In response Sarat Bose replied, 'Jawahar, I don't believe the crash story. Subhas never wore such a watch. He wore one with a round dial that mother had given him.'

Writing in the 20 April 2015 issue of *India Today* magazine, journalist Sandeep Unnithan says, 'For two decades between 1948 and 1968, Government of India placed Bose family members under intensive surveillance. Sleuths intercepted, read and recorded letters of Bose families exactly in the same way that they would of relatives and contacts of terrorists.' The same report pointed out that the man behind all this was IB director Bhola Nath Mullick. He shared the letters with M.L. Hooja who became the IB chief in 1968 and Rameshwar Nath Kao who went on to be the first Secretary of the Research and Analysis Wing (RAW) when it was formed. All the files containing the details of the snooping were marked 'top secret' and 'very secret'.

A good example of putting the lid on any information going out to the public on Netaji's whereabouts is provided by the case of Ardhendu Sarkar, a mechanical engineer with the Ranchi-based public sector Heavy Engineering Corporation (HEC). In 1962 Sarkar was sent on deputation to the Gorlovka Machine Building plant in Ukraine (which is now an independent country but was then part of the Soviet Union). Here he met a German called Zerovin employed there. Zerovin told Sarkar that he had met Netaji in a gulag in 1947–48 and they had even exchanged a few words in German. Zerovin had been sent to the gulag for indoctrination. An excited Sarkar, on the first available opportunity, rushed to Moscow and the Indian Embassy. If Sarkar had thought that the officials there would be equally excited he was mistaken. He was reprimanded and asked to shut up. 'Why have you come to this country? Does your assignment involve poking your nose into politics? Don't share this information with anyone. Just do what you are sent for,' Ardhendu Sarkar was told. A few days later Sarkar was repatriated back home. A shaken Sarkar narrated these facts only in 2000 in his deposition before the Mukherjee Commission.

The government continued to insist that Netaji had in fact died in the air crash and went to ridiculous lengths to prove this. Not only were two pre-biased commissions of inquiry (Shah Nawaz and Khosla) set up to prove his death, the government was going ballistic even in the early 1990s. In the 1980s the government's intelligence wing trained their sights on Gumnami Baba's visitors and even trying to dissuade curious analysts from calling on him. V.N. Arora of Faizabad who has been quoted in an earlier chapter reveals that one day, out of curiosity—this was sometime in the year 1980—he had decided to call on Gumnami Baba. He was told to come the following day at 4 pm. The next day, an intelligence official dropped into his house in the afternoon, enquiring why he wanted to meet Baba. Not only this, he insisted on sitting with Arora till late in the evening so that Arora could not step out of the house. 'How did they know that I was to meet Baba? Obviously they were keeping tabs on who ever visited his house,' Arora says, pointing out that Gumnami Baba, in those days was living in a dilapidated building that had no electricity.

The P.V. Narasimha Rao government which came to power in 1991 tried hard to convince Emilie Schenkl, Subhas Chandra Bose's wife and other family members that he had in fact died in an air crash and therefore sought their consent to bring home the ashes of Netaji kept in the Renkoji Temple in Tokyo. The desperation is obvious going by the notes written on file by the Union home secretary, K. Padmanabhaiah. He noted, 'It would therefore be necessary to take the members of Netaji's family into confidence in the first place by convincing them as to the genuineness of the ashes. It should be then easier to handle opposition from other quarters like the Forward Bloc.' The note went on to add, 'Netaji's wife and daughter are at present in Augsburg, Germany. It is felt that they can be approached through another nephew of Netaji, Dr Sisir Bose. Shri Amiya Nath Bose, the most vociferous sceptic of the air crash theory, needs to be brought around by approaching at an appropriately high level. There is a good chance that if reasonably approached, the family members may drop their opposition. The question of an appropriate memorial involving the mortal remains shall also have to be addressed in due course.'

When this writer asked K. Padmanabhaiah the basis on which he was so sanguine that the ashes were that of Netaji, he pleaded that the event was two decades old and he did not remember the exact sequence of events. 'Some materials were brought before me on which I based my note. What the contents were, I do not remember now,' the retired home secretary said.

The zealousness of the government to prove that Netaji had died in an air crash was presumably because of the fear that declassification of records in Russia might lead to the truth tumbling out. As is known, the Soviet Union broke up after 1991 in the wake of glasnost or openness. In this scenario many secret archives were expected to be thrown open. The panic in the Indian establishment is clear after *Asia and Africa Today*, a journal brought out by the Oriental Institute in Moscow announced in 1993 that it would publish some material relating to Subhas Chandra Bose which was culled from the archives of the KGB. Probably at the behest of none other than Prime Minister P.V. Narasimha Rao, the Indian ambassador to Russia, Ronen Sen tried to use diplomatic pressure on the Institute to stop the article from being published. A counsellor of the embassy, Ajay Malhotra went to meet the deputy chief editor of the magazine V.K. Tourdjev to prevail upon him to refrain from publishing any such article.

Taking advantage of the more open (or probably less closed) regime in Russia a team of scholars from the Asiatic Society of Kolkata (that had an agreement with the Oriental Institute in Moscow) went down to access possible files relating to Indo-Soviet relations and about Netaji. In the course of the visit the team realized that only after examining the KGB archives could they conclusively say anything. They also realized that the KGB archives could possibly be opened up only on the request of the Government of India. Thus on their return they moved the Ministry of External Affairs. The joint secretary (East Europe), R.L. Narayan then wrote a note to the Foreign Secretary on 12 January 1996 that the Indian ambassador in Russia could issue a *demarche* to the Russian government to organize a search of the KGB archives. This was because an earlier request from the Government of India had elicited a negative response that there was nothing in Russian records on that matter. A *demarche* in diplomatic terms is a strong request and the word is used to convey the importance of the request.

The earlier request had been place in January 1992 when Russia was beginning to open up. In fact in his note, Narayan wrote, 'In January 1992 we had received a disclaimer from the Russian foreign ministry that said that according to the Republican archives no information whatsoever was available on the stay of Subhas Chandra Bose in Soviet Union in 1945 and thereafter.' In the same note Narayan had suggested that the Russian disclaimer was possibly based on the archives of the post-Stalin period (post-1953). Narayan had said that since it would be unrealistic to expect that Russian authorities would allow Indian scholars access to KGB archives, the Indian government could 'request Russian authorities to conduct a search themselves into the archives and let us know if there is any evidence of Netaji's stay in the Soviet Union.'

When the file went up to foreign minister, Pranab Mukherjee he called for an urgent meeting on 14 January. The move for the *demarche* was dropped. On 7 March, the same joint secretary wrote to the foreign secretary once again. This time he wrote that a formal request to the Russian government may be misunderstood by the latter and therefore he recommended that the Asiatic Society itself should be allowed to pursue the matter independently with the Oriental Institute.

Close to the elections, politicians become very agreeable. Thus the same Narasimha Rao whose government had actively thwarted any attempt to get information out of Russia on 25 March 1996 advised his joint secretary to pursue the matter. The joint secretary wrote to the foreign secretary, 'PM would like our ambassador in Moscow to make discreet enquiries at a high level to ascertain, if possible, the existence of such information in Russia and the possible reaction of the Russian side. Foreign secretary may see.' What happened to this discreet enquiry is not known.

The paranoia about Netaji continued even after the Congress government bowed out of office. In 1999, the National Democratic Alliance (NDA) government under Atal Bihari Vajpayee set up the Mukherjee Commission to inquire about the disappearance of Netaji.

This was after a judgment by the Chief Justice of Calcutta High Court, Prabha Shankar Mishra. But the NDA government showed little keenness to cooperate with the Commission. When the Commission asked the government to share files relating to Netaji in its possession, the reply was tantamount to a flat no. The home secretary, Kamal Pande filed an affidavit and wrote back, 'I have carefully examined the documents and I am bona fide satisfied that the disclosure of these documents would also hurt the sentiments of the public at large and may evoke wide spread reactions as these documents if disclosed may lower the image of Netaji Subhas Chandra Bose. Diplomatic relations with friendly countries may also be adversely affected if the said documents are disclosed. In these circumstances I withhold permission to produce the said records or to release their contents or give any evidence derived therefrom and claim privileges under section 123and 124 of Evidence Act.' Pande also said, 'The disclosure of the records would also be violating the mandatory provisions of Article 74(2) of the Constitution in as much as the records ordered to be produced also belong to the class of documents which it is the practice to keep secret and ensuring the proper functioning of public service. The records include notes and minutes by officers and ministers on file.'

The government's reluctance to open the Netaji files continued even after the installation of Narendra Modi as prime minister in 2014. When Trinamool Congress Rajya Sabha MP Sukhendu Shekhar Roy asked the home minister, Rajnath Singh when the files that the government had on Netaji would be opened, the minister of state for home, Haribhai Chaudhary replied—on 17 December 2014—that there were fifty-eight files with the Prime Minister's Office and twenty-nine files with the external affairs ministry. The minister said that the government had no plans to declassify any of these files because their contents were of a 'sensitive nature' and could lead to problems in 'India's relations with other countries.' In an RTI reply, the Prime Minister's Office also refused to declassify the files arguing that 'the disclosures would prejudicially affect relations with foreign countries.'

A recent RTI query by a freelance journalist Choodamani Nagendra, seeking to know whether the GOI had any records relating to Subhas Bose being declared as a war criminal and what steps the government had taken to get his name removed from this list, has drawn a blank. The home ministry to whom this query was directed ducked the query citing some obsolete governmental provisions not to make public this information. This was before Modi met Netaji's family members and announced his decision to open the files.

However many people, including Netaji's family members feel that there is no harm in declassifying the files now, after so many years. This is true. Even if the files were to indicate that Stalin killed Netaji or the British got hold of Netaji and liquidated him or even if it was found that the Japanese had secretly surrendered Netaji to the Allied powers, this would hardly spoil relations with the present leaders of these countries. For any misdemeanour of Stalin, Indians are not likely to have an adverse opinion of the Vladimir Putin regime in Russia or for that matter of the present heads of state in the UK and Germany.

In fact the people of India and Netaji lovers aver that the files relating to Netaji are not being opened because they contain information that would portray leaders like Jawaharlal Nehru and Indira Gandhi in poor light. In a way Kamal Pande's affidavit brought the cat out of the bag by pointing out that the files could not be declassified because it had annotations by ministers and officials. In other words the then home secretary was scared of what opinions Nehru and his mandarins had of Netaji. The revelations would adversely affect the image of Nehru and his close circle, and not of Netaji as Kamal Pande made out. It is also possible that the declassification of the files would bring out more instances of the government's eavesdropping on Netaji's relatives. Official sources also aver that intelligence officials in their various reports in the past have demonised Netaji and this would also become public. For instance intelligence reports claim that Bose never married Emilie Schenkl and she was just his live-in partner. Moreover Netaji had a passionate affair with a lady politician from Bengal and later with someone in Burma. Most of them are based on hearsay and have no bearing with reality. These reports were just to character assassinate Subhas Bose and to portray him poorly vis-à-vis Congress politicians like Nehru who came to rule the country after Independence.

That is why Netaji's family members and other Netaji lovers (and there are innumerable such people) feel that Narendra Modi has no vested interest and will not go back on his promise to declassify the relevant files. A small step was taken by the government in this matter in mid-April after a ruckus was created when the contents of two declassified files revealed that Netaji's kin had been being tailed for twenty long years. An inter-ministerial committee headed by the Cabinet Secretary was set up to review the Netaji files and their contents in the light of the Official Secrets Act. The Committee will decide whether these files can be opened up and will start the process on 23 January 2016. Incidentally the rules specify that files can be declassified after thirty years. This means that files earlier than 1985 can be declassified.

The million dollar question: will the committee recommend declassification? But a word of caution: declassification of the files may illustrate in detail the attitude of successive Indian regimes towards Netaji but may not throw light on his whereabouts. A former top official of the intelligence department who served for four decades in both the IB and RAW says that all that may be found in the files would be cross-references to what is contained in files in other countries like Japan, United Kingdom and perhaps the Soviet Union.

About the Author

Kingshuk Nag is Resident Editor, *The Times of India* in Hyderabad, a position he has held from July 2005. The *ToI* attained the position of largest circulated English daily in Hyderabad during his tenure. A recipient of the prestigious Prem Bhatia Award for Excellence in Political Reporting and Analyses for his publication's coverage of the 2002 communal riots in Gujarat while he was stationed in Ahmedabad, **Nag** is a hard-nosed 24X7 journalist, ever ready to receive the proverbial tip-off on a story even if it means a colleague calling him at midnight to inform him of a news break. Probably his finest hour as a journalist and editor, the reports carried by the *ToI* on the unprecedented riots—in the face of confrontation with the authorities and despite personal threats—went a long way in curbing the conflagration. Of the three decades he has spent as a journalist, **Nag** has served with the *ToI* for twenty-two years and held positions such as that of Resident Editor at Ahmedabad (May 2000 – June 2005), Business Editor (South) based out of Bengaluru (January 1998 – April 2000) and Chief of Business Bureau at New Delhi (June 1993 – December 1997). **Nag** is also a recipient of the state-level Rajiv Gandhi Sadbhavana Award—2010 given by the Rajiv Gandhi Forum of Odisha.

Nag is an alumnus of the 1980 batch of the Delhi School of Economics, University of Delhi. Before he entered journalism, he learnt about market economics during a two-year stint with the Tata Economic Consultancy Services in Mumbai. He returned to Delhi, the city that he had grown up in, to work with the Associated Chambers of Commerce and Industry of India (Assocham). Thereafter, he entered journalism full-time, starting his career with *Business India* magazine.

Nag has written a book titled *Saffron Tide* that traces the growth of the Bharatiya Janata Party. In 2013, in the run-up to the national elections he penned *NaMo Story*, a biography of Narendra Modi. The book received rave reviews for providing an objective view of the politician and is by far the highest selling book on India's current Prime Minister. **Nag's** second book named *Battleground Telangana*, released in mid-2011, charts out the fifty-year-old history of the conflict for a new state that came into being in June 2014. His first book, also written during his tenure in Hyderabad, is called *Double Life of Ramalinga Raju: The Story of India's Largest Corporate Scam*. The book, which won critical acclaim and became a bestseller, explored the motivations that turned the information technology czar into a scamster in the process running to the ground a global computer software company.

Nag is currently researching the idea of whether economic reforms without political reforms have been disastrous for India. A public interest litigation (PIL) petition filed by him in the Hyderabad High Court is seeking far-reaching political reforms.

The motto of the school where he studied, the Frank Anthony Public School in New Delhi, 'Courage is Destiny' is his credo and continues to influence him.